17975

D1206450

AN INTRODUCTION TO COMMUNISM

An Introduction to Communism

by

Henlee H. Barnette

BAKER BOOK HOUSE
Grand Rapids, Michigan
1964

PHOTOLITHOPRINTED BY CUSHING - MALLOY, INC.
ANN ARBOR, MICHIGAN, UNITED STATES OF AMERICA
1964

To
John

ACKNOWLEDGMENTS

Grateful acknowledgment is made to the following publishers and authors for permission to quote from works cited.

Association Press, Karl Barth and Johannes Hamel, *How to Serve God in a Marxist Land*, New York, 1959.

Broadman Press, W. O. Carver, *The Acts of the Apostles*, Nashville, Tennessee, 1961.

Christian Century, September 8, 1948.

Christianity Today, December 21, 1962.

The Works of Plato, tr. by Benjamin Jowett in *Communism: Aims and Advance*, reprinted by permission of Dial Press, Inc.

Wm. B. Eerdmans Publishing Company, Lester DeKoster, *Communism and Christian Faith*, Grand Rapids, Mich., 1962.

Marx and Engels Basic Writings on Politics and Philosophy, Lewis S. Feuer, ed., Doubleday, Inc., Anchor Books, New York, 1959.

International Publishers, Lenin, *Selected Works*, by permission of International Publishers Company, Inc., New York; also, Karl Marx, *Selected Works*, 1932, Vol. I, pp. 16-18; Karl Marx, "Critique of the Gotha Programme," *Selected Works*, Vol. II, 1938, p. 565; Friedrich Engels, *Anti-Duhring*, Marxist Library, n.d. Vol. XVIII, p. 109.

Harper and Row, for quotes from Elton Trueblood, *Alternative to Futility*, New York, 1948; Richard Crossman, ed., *The God That Failed*, 1951; Leon Trotsky, *Stalin*, 1941.

Life, October 24, 1961.

National Council of Churches of Christ in the U.S.A. for permission to quote from the Revised Standard Version of the Bible.

Philosophical Library, Inc., Karl Barth, *Against the Stream: Shorter Post-War Writings, 1946-52*, New York, 1954.

University of Michigan Press, Nicolas Berdyaev, *The Russian Revolution*, Ann Arbor, Michigan, 1961.

The Westminster Press, *Communism and the Theologians: Study of an Encounter*, Charles West, © SCM Press, Ltd., 1958, published in the U.S.A. by The Westminster Press, 1958.

PREFACE

Communism continues to be both a threat and a challenge to the free world. Its threat is seen in continuous expansion in the areas where least expected, such as Cuba and Northern India. This expansion is carried out by means of a "salami strategy" —just enough is sliced off short of provoking a nuclear war. Evidence now points to a serious Communist effort to take by piecemeal all of South America.

Communism's challenge to the West appears at numerous levels in such aspects as economic and educational development, scientific advance, missionary and evangelistic zeal, a world view, and total commitment.

An enormous amount of literature about Communism has come from the press during the last decade. Much of it generates more heat than light about the subject. The issue is so explosive that one has to muster all of his powers to be objective and dispassionate about it. I have sought to maintain such an attitude in this work. The reader can judge for himself as to what extent I have achieved this aim.

The purpose of this book is to present in non-technical terms an analysis of the Communist-Christian encounter, and to suggest guidelines for Christian action in meeting Communism's challenge. Primary sources in English have been used exclusively in dealing with Communist doctrines. In the case of interpretative materials, I have sought to rely on sources generally acknowledged as solid ones. Some information is derived from personal impressions received while visiting in the Soviet Union.

Chapter One attempts to define Communism, state its goals and to what extent these goals have been achieved in the world today. Brief portraits of the dynamic personalities in the Communist movement are presented in Chapter Two. Basic dogmas and doctrines of Marxism-Leninism are described in Chapter Three. Briefs of Communism, pro and con, are set forth in Chapters Four and Five with the view to evaluating its strength and weakness. Chapter Six is devoted to a description and evaluation of certain leading theologians' responses to Communism, and suggestions toward a more realistic theological posture. The final chapter describes specific aspects of the Communist thrust which challenge Christian forces and suggests a strategy of action for combatting Communism.

A bibliography appears at the end of the book for those who desire to probe deeper into the problem of Communism.

I am grateful to Helen, my helpmeet, for reading the manuscript, and making corrections and suggestions for improvement in style. She is absolved, however, from all responsibility for the opinions I express.

To all others who have indirectly contributed to my thoughts on Communism, I wish now to express my thanks. Frequent footnotes testify of my effort to acknowledge help from other authors. It is impossible to acknowledge all sources of help in writing a book.

This is the third manuscript that Mrs. Glenn Hinson has typed for me. In each instance I owe her a particular debt of gratitude for her patience and efficiency.

Henlee H. Barnette

Southern Baptist Theological Seminary
Louisville, Kentucky
February, 1964

CONTENTS

CHAPTER I

Communism's Aims and Advance

"Let's see how the world is going today." These words were uttered by a four-year-old as she strode toward a chapel window, symbolizing the world. It does not take a prophet's insight to see that the world is going into the Communist camp at an alarming pace. What is the nature of communism, its aims, and what significant advances has it made in terms of world conquest? And what is the free world doing to arrest the Communist world movement? These are the questions considered in this chapter.

1. What Is Communism?

• Communism may be broadly defined as any social system in which all property is held in common. That is to say, that all goods are owned by all the people of a community or country.

• As an ideal, communism roots in the very beginning of Western culture. Plato (427?-347 B.C.) advocated a limited form of communism in his famous work, *The Republic*. He envisioned three classes in the ideal republic: guardians (a small group of highly trained rulers); auxiliaries (a skilled professional army); and the civilian masses. The rulers and soldiers were not to possess property because it tends to corrupt those in power.[1] Hence, they were to live in communal relations.

In this instance Plato is describing a form of communal life for only two groups in society: rulers and soldiers. Dean Inge goes so far as to declare that "the so-called communism of Plato had nothing to do with economics" and that it was "a desperate attempt to devise a system of government which would be efficient and honest."[2] Thus, Plato was not a communist before Karl Marx, but a philosopher concerned with giving the power

[1]*The Works of Plato*, trans. by Benjamin Jowett. New York: Dial Press n.d., "The Republic," Book III, pp. 131-132.

[2]W. R. Inge, "The Christian Tradition," in *Christianity and Communism*, edited by H. Wilson Harris. Boston: Marshall Jones Co., 1937, p. 15.

to rule to men who would have no opportunity to feather their own nests.

In his old age, Plato did dream of an ideal "communist" state for all its citizens described as follows:

> The first and highest form of the state and of the government and of the law is that in which there prevails most widely the ancient saying, that "Friends have all things in common." Whether there is now, or ever will be, this communion of women and children and of property in which the private and individual is altogether banished from life, and things which are by nature private, such as eyes, and ears, and hands, have become common, and in some way see and hear and act in common, and all men express praise and blame, and feel joy and sorrow, on the same occasions, and the laws unite the city to the utmost,—whether all this is possible or not, I say that no man, acting upon any other principle, will ever constitute a state more exalted in virtue, or truer and better than this. Such a state, whether inhabited by Gods, or sons of Gods, will make them blessed who dwell therein; and therefore to this we are to look for the pattern of the state, and to cling to this, and, as far as possible, to seek for one which is like this.[3]

* With political realism, Aristotle (384-322 B.C.) criticizes Plato's theory of a communist state, noting that private property is essential to happiness and to the development of the virtue of generosity. His most telling stricture, however, is in pointing out that the evils which arise out of the possession of private property are due to a very different cause—the wickedness of human nature.[4] And by implication he indicates that the same evils would prevail to a greater degree in a communist society.

In succeeding centuries "communistic" communities have appeared. The Essenes possessed a form of communal life. Josephus refers to these people, numbering about four thousand and living in small communities along the Dead Sea. They despised riches and there was a law among them that "those who come to them must let what they have be common to the whole order . . .

[3]*The Works of Plato, op. cit.,* "Laws," Book V, pp. 433-434.
[4]Aristotle, *Politics,* trans. by Benjamin Jowett. New York: Modern Library, 1943, Book II, Chapter 5, 15.

everyone's possessions are intermingled with every other's possessions."[5]

The primitive Christian church witnessed a unique type of communal life in Jerusalem described as follows:

> And fear came upon every soul; and many wonders and signs were done through the apostles. And all who believed were together and had all things in common; and they sold their possessions and goods and distributed them to all, as any had need (Acts 2:43-45, RSV).
> Now the company of those who believed were of one heart and soul, and no one said that any of the things which he possessed was his own, but they had everything in common. And with great power the apostles gave their testimony to the resurrection of the Lord Jesus, and great grace was upon them all. There was not a needy person among them, for as many as were possessors of lands or houses sold them, and brought the proceeds of what was sold and laid it at the apostles' feet; and distribution was made to each as any had need (Acts 4:32-35, RSV).

Several facts should be noted in this so-called "communistic experiment." It was a voluntary and spontaneous expression of brotherly love among Christians. There was no coercion of membership or confiscation of property. Peter's rebuke of Ananias is sufficient evidence that the sharing of goods was voluntary. He says: "While it remained unsold, did it not remain your own? And after it was sold, was it not at your disposal?" (Acts 5:4 RSV).

W. O. Carver puts the whole problem in the right perspective when he declares:

> It was not communism, nor a general distribution of goods. The tenses are imperfect. The sales of real estate and of personal property were made by the owners from time to time and the distribution was made on the basis of need as the need developed. The great number of "sojourners" in their company in part ac-

[5]William Whiston, *The Life and Works of Flavius Josephus*. Philadelphia: John C. Winston Co., "Wars of the Jews," Book 2, Chapter 8, pp. 673-674.

counts for this, and the fact that the first converts included so
largely the poor. Conditions were abnormal in Jerusalem.[6]

As the church grew in numbers, the "common fund" at Jerusalem became impractical and was replaced by a "poor fund"
(Acts 6:1-6). Thus the "poor fund" became the pattern of the
growing church. Paul contributed to this fund and specified reg-
ulations for the administration of widow's pensions (I Timothy
5:16).

Taking the *koinonia* of the early church at Jerusalem as a
prototype, a few Christians through the centuries have attempted
to develop similar communities. In the twelfth century, religious
sects imitated the early Christians, developing communal pat-
terns of living. Among these were the Waldensians, Albigensians
and the radical wing of the Anabaptists. During the nineteenth
century in America the Shakers, the Mennonites, and others
sought to live a "communistic" type of life. Only a few experiments of this kind exist today. Among these is the Koinonia Farm
established by Clarence Jordan near Americus, Georgia.

In addition to the religious communistic communities, numerous secular experiments have appeared from time to time in
America. The New Harmony experiment, New Harmony, Indiana
(1826), the Brooks Farm (1841-1847) in West Roxbury, Massachusetts, and the Oneida Community in Oneida, New York, are
among the most famous.

Contemporary communism, Soviet style, is radically different
from any of the types we have examined. Communism today is a
world-wide conspiracy which seeks to establish a society in which
everything is owned and controlled by the government, based
upon a materialistic view of all reality derived from the atheistic
philosophy of Karl Marx, implemented by the revolutionary
tactics of V. I. Lenin, and directed by a small dedicated and
dictatorial political party.

It should be noted here that communism is different from
socialism. Socialism, as it now exists in countries such as
Sweden, calls for the socialization of only the major natural
resources and means of production and distribution. Soviet com-

[6]*The Acts of the Apostles.* Nashville: Broadman Press, 1916, p. 35.

munism, on the other hand, demands the complete socialization of all natural resources, means of production, communication, distribution and consumption. Socialism is established through democratic means, whereas communism is set up and maintained by force, military power, secret police, false propaganda, persecution, and murder.

2. Communist Aims

As has been stated, communism is a world movement seeking to communize all nations. Its central aim is to draw and to drive every country on earth into the communist camp. The spirit of global conquest is expressed in every thought and action of the communists. From the founding father and apostles of communism came statements of world conquest. Karl Marx, father of modern communism, declared, in 1848, that the communists "have a world to win."[7] V. I. Lenin, father of the communist revolution in Russia, asserted: "As long as capitalism and socialism exist, we cannot live in peace: in the end, one or the other will triumph—a funeral dirge will be sung either over the Soviet Republic or over the world of capitalism."[8] Joseph Stalin in 1927 prophesied that there would be two world centers (Communist East and Capitalist West) and that the struggle between them would "decide the fate of Capitalism and Socialism throughout the world."[9]

At a Kremlin reception on November 17, 1956, Khrushchev was overheard to say: "If you don't like us, don't accept our invitations, and don't invite us to come to see you. Whether you like it or not history is on our side. We will bury you!"[10] By this statement, of course, he meant that the non-communist world will give way to the march of history which is supposedly moving in-

[7]*The Communist Manifesto.*

[8]*Selected Works.* New York: International Publishers, 1943, Vol. VIII, p. 297.

[9]*Works.* Moscow: Foreign Languages Publishing House, 1954, Vol. X, pp. 140-141.

[10]Department of State, *Soviet World Outlook,* Department of State Publication 6836, U. S. Government Office. Washington, D. C.: 1951, "Foreword."

evitably toward a communist world. And in a television program addressed to an American audience (1957) Khrushchev confidently declared: "Your grandchildren will live under socialism."

Obviously the United States is included in the communist blueprint of conquest. William Z. Foster, former chairman of the Communist Party of the United States, in a sworn statement declared:

> When a Communist heads the government of the United States —and that day will come just as surely as the sun rises—the government will not be a capitalist government but a Soviet government, and behind this government will stand the Red army to enforce the dictatorship of the proletariat.[11]

Global conquest is expressed in communist literature, art, movies, plays, music, and song. This writer was awakened at 5:00 a.m. by the sound of marching feet and fierce singing of hundreds of young Russians on the streets of Kiev in the Ukraine. Passionately they sang the International, the anthem of world communism which declares in part:

> Arise, you prisoners of starvation!
> Arise, you wretched of the earth,
> For justice thunders condemnation
> A better world's in birth.
>
> *Chorus*:
> 'Tis the final conflict,
> Let each stand in his place;
> The International Soviet
> Shall be the human race.

Let no one be so naive as to think that the communists will be satisfied with their present gains. A blueprint for taking over the world has already been drawn up and persistent efforts will be expanded to sovietize every nation. Only those ignorant of communist ideology and tactics could believe otherwise.

[11]*100 Things You Should Know About Communism*, Committee on Un-American Activities, Washington, D. C.: August 15, 1949, p. 4.

3. Communism's Advance

Communism's advancement toward its goal of world conquest is incredible. In less than forty-five years the communists have captured approximately one-fourth of the earth's surface and now control about one billion people. Millions of people may yet go into the communist camp.

Beginning with the Bolshevik revolution of October, 1917, when Lenin took over the Russian government, the communists have been tireless and persistent in their efforts to extend communist influence within and without Russia. In 1918 Lenin established the Russian Socialist Federated Soviet Republic, the heart of the Soviet Union. Thereafter, the communists of Russia incorporated fourteen other republics to become the Union of Soviet Socialist Republics (USSR).

At the end of World War II, the Russians got the opportunity they had been waiting for. In May, 1945, Soviet troops occupied a total of what had been ten independent states of Europe. These countries were Finland, Estonia, Latvia, Lithuania, Poland, Czechoslovakia, Hungary, Romania, Bulgaria, and Albania. In addition parts of Germany, Austria, and Norway, including the island of Bornholm, were in Soviet hands. Soviet troops were also in Yugoslavia, but Tito, the dictator, was able to oust them and to set up his own brand of communism.

Of the captive nations, Finland, Norway, Bornholm, and Austria became free of Soviet occupation at a terrible cost in terms of reparations. This left the Soviets in complete control of most of Eastern Europe. Those countries annexed by the Russians are called "satellites" because they have been drawn into the Soviet orbit of control and have become dependent upon the USSR.

Where the Soviets could not take over by military might, they extended their influence by infiltration. Large communist parties responsive to International Communism with control from Moscow exist in Italy and France. In Italy in 1948, the communists gained almost one-fourth of the seats in the Chamber of Deputies and in 1959 made even greater gains. In 1956 in

France, the Communist Party polled the largest number of votes of any one political party.

Communists began to infiltrate China in the 1920's. Soviet agents helped to set up the Communist Party. By 1949 this nation of more than six hundred million people was completely in the hands of the communists headed by Mao Tse-tung.

Today all of Africa is a prime target of Soviet communists. Efforts are being made by the Kremlin to secure a base in Africa for sovietizing all of the "Dark Continent."

Communists are also concentrating on capturing all of Latin America. Every country in South America is infiltrated with communists, waiting for the opportunity to seize governments. It should be recalled that Guatemala fell into the hands of the communists in 1950, but they were later forced out of power. But such misfortunes do not deter the communists who wait even now for the chance to regain power in Guatemala and eventually to control all Latin countries.

Cuba, just ninety miles off the coast of Florida, fell into the hands of Fidel Castro and his rebels in 1959. What appeared to be a healthy revolution has fallen into the control of key communist leaders, among them agents from both Russia and China. Cubans were told in the beginning of the revolution that the new government would stand for freedom and democracy. First to be eliminated were the supporters of Batista, ousted dictator; then went the free press. Farms were collectivized and industries confiscated, many of them properties of Americans. Hundreds of "counter-revolutionaries" were imprisoned and liquidated. The whole pattern of action by the new government conforms to the communist strategy in other countries. Cuba has now become a launching pad for the Soviets to sovietize all Latin America.

In 1963 the free world was shocked to discover that Khrushchev had placed a number of long-range missiles on Cuba aimed at the U.S. A blockade of Cuba was established and Khrushchev was forced to remove the missiles under threat of war from the U.S. government. However, several thousands of Russian troops remain in Cuba. Also hundreds of students from South America are in Cuban schools receiving training in revolutionary tactics to be used in establishing communist governments in their respective countries.

The U.S.A. has long been a target of Soviet communism. Since the founding of the Communist Party in this country, the movement has been under the control of Moscow. The Party's avowed aim is to sovietize the U.S. and to make it one of the republics of a world-wide Soviet system.

By 1961 the Communist Party had grown to a membership of approximately 40 million, according to the report of the 22nd Congress of the Communist Party. China had the largest party with 17 million. The official claim of the USSR, October 20, 1961, was that of 8,872,516 members with 843,489 candidates for Party membership. Thus, the Party constitutes about 7% of the adult population. The largest parties outside the Soviet bloc in 1961 were Indonesia with 1,750,000 and Italy with about 1,200,000. Even Cuba boasted during this year a Party membership of 27,000,000, about four times that of the U.S. Communist Party.[12]

4. Counter-Action of Free Nations

While the communist octopus has been engulfing the earth with its cruel tentacles of intrigue, false propaganda, brutality, and military might, free nations have taken steps to stop the beast. When the West became convinced that the Russians had no intentions of negotiating a peaceful settlement in connection with the captive European nations, the Cold War began.

It must be recalled that when the Nazis invaded Russia, Stalin turned to the Western allies for help which he received in terms of enormous quantities of food, clothing, ships, tanks, planes, munitions. Russia became an ally with the Western powers. Even before the war was won, free nations organized the United Nations at San Francisco in 1945, including Russia as a member.

For a brief period after the war, hope mounted for a just and lasting peace. Unfortunately the U.N. was unable to bring about disarmament or to resolve disputes among the nations.

[12]For further facts on Communist Party strength see *World Strength of the Communist Party*. Bureau of Intelligence and Research, State Department, Washington, D. C., January, 1962.

Instead of disarming as all nations had agreed to do, Russia maintained a huge military force and kept Eastern European nations under her control. Soviet representatives in the U.N. were sucessful in blocking any attempt to settle differences between nations.

In order to stop communist agression, the Western powers began to re-arm and to form alliances. Twenty-one Latin American nations, including the U.S., formed the Organization of American States (OAS) in 1948. In the same year the U.S. and Great Britain, along with ten other nations bordering on the North Atlantic Ocean, formed the North Atlantic Treaty Organization (NATO). Defense alliances were also formed by the U.S. with the Republic of China on Formosa, South Korea, and with Japan. In 1954 the Southeast Asia Treaty Organization (SEATO) was formed which included the U.S., Great Britain, France, the Philippine Republic, Australia, New Zealand, Thailand, and Pakistan. In 1955 the Baghdad Pact or Middle East Treaty Organization came into existence with Great Britain, Turkey, Iraq, Iran, and Pakistan as participants.

The U.N. has not been wholly successful in bringing about peace, but does have some achievements in this area to its credit. In 1946 it was instrumental in securing the withdrawal of Soviet troops from Iran, and in 1950 successfully contributed to the solution of the Korean crisis in which the South Koreans were freed from communist invaders.

In 1945 the Western nations began a series of conferences with the communists in hopes of achieving peace. In that year the Potsdam Agreement, which called for a series of meetings of foreign ministers of Russia and the Western nations, was established. At the top of the agenda was the unification of Germany. After six conferences, no agreement had been reached due to Russia's insistence that Germany should be kept unarmed and neutral, without membership in any Western alliances. It was felt by representatives of the Western nations that, without defenses, Germany would become another victim of Soviet aggression.

In 1955 Western and Communist representatives achieved a treaty on Austria, which left the country neutral and without the privilege of entering into any defense alliance with the West.

During the same year the "Big Four" powers—U.S., Great Britain, France, and Soviet Union—sent their heads of states (Eisenhower, Eden, Faure, Khrushchev, and Bulganin) to a so-called "summit conference" held at Geneva, Switzerland, and later in London, to work out a unification of Germany. No settlement was reached and to this day Germany remains divided into East and West Germany.

Nikita Khrushchev wrecked the "Paris Conference" alleging that the United States was guilty of aggression, citing the U-2 incident as an example. Because President Eisenhower refused to apologize for this incident, Khrushchev refused to enter into any negotiations at the Paris Conference.

Many representatives of Western nations now feel that negotiations with the USSR are useless. Russia has consistently refused to negotiate in good faith, preferring to sustain the cold war to her own political advantage. Since World War I she has already violated more than three hundred treaties and has pursued a policy of aggression. At the same time Khrushchev has talked of "peaceful co-existence," that is, that communists and free people can exist peacefully side by side in the same world. So-called "neutralist nations" as Sweden, Switzerland, India, Burma, Indonesia, most of the Arab nations, have been inclined to accept the peaceful coexistence doctrine. But the scrapping of international agreements by Russia and continual interference in other governments have left most free nations skeptical of any proposals for peace.

In addition to the formation of alliances with other countries, the U.S. has led in providing economic support and technical help to needy and underdeveloped countries. Two of the most effective weapons against communism are the Marshall Plan and the Peace Corps. The former aided Europe in getting back on her feet economically after World War II, and the latter is helping underdeveloped countries to help themselves on the road to economic and technical progress.

5. Communism's Prospects

Communists are optimistic about the future. Convinced that history is on their side, they look for the imminent downfall of "decadent" capitalistic countries and enthronement of socialism. A visitor to the Soviet Union is immediately struck by an optimism which radiates from the faces of the people. Their belief that history is on their side coupled with success in so many nations has convinced the communists that it is only a matter of time until socialism will become world-wide. Like vultures the communists wait to feast upon the Capitalist carcass now allegedly in its death throes.

It appears that the West is losing the war against communism. This is due, in part, to the fact that the Free World has not yet become aware that it is in a world war.[13] Of course, the communists have not openly declared war on the West. Rather, they have been the pretenders of peace. But, to the communists, peace is war conducted by "other than military means." As early as 1928 Stalin declared that there is no contradiction between Russia's preparation for revolutionary war and a consistent policy of peace. Revolutionary war, he maintained, is but "a continuation of revolutionary peace policy, 'by other means.' "[14] In other words, "hot" and "cold" are phases of the same war. It is a persistent and protracted battle in which every weapon is employed—the U.N., diplomacy, science, art, music, economics, psychology, propaganda, sabotage, subversion, military power, as parts of a total strategy for communist conquest. As Bertram Wolfe has pointed out, the communists know that they are engaged in a war to the finish, a war for the world . . . . Every separate issue, every negotiation, every conference, every utterance they regard as a move in that war, whereas for us in the West each is treated as a separate concrete issue to be settled once and for all in order that we may relax."[15]

Until the free world understands the nature of Red warfare, it will go on losing the battle. In the past Americans have gone to the battle fronts with the idea of winning the war, getting back home, and resuming normal life. Communism cannot be de-

[13]See Robert Strausz-Hupé, *et al., Protracted Conflict.* New York: Harper and Brothers, 1960, where it is contended that the communists are scoring victories in this war because they know they are in it.

[14]*International Press Conferences.* Vol. 8, No. 84, November 28, 1928, p. 1590.

[15]*Life,* October 20, 1961, p. 134.

feated in this fashion. It has many fronts and must be fought on a global scale. Every weapon at hand must be utilized in the struggle.

While the hour is late, it is not too late to win against communism. The tide of the battle will turn when the peoples of free nations become aware of the real threat of communism and develop a positive program to meet it. Attempts to "stop" communism by containment are not enough. The West must seize the initiative, assume a positive stance, and adopt a realistic policy of justice and freedom, if the communist conspiracy is to be repulsed.

CHAPTER II

Men behind the Movement

One cannot fully understand a movement without some knowledge of the men behind it. Therefore, to understand the nature of contemporary communism, it is necessary to become acquainted with the man who "thought it up" and his disciples who put it into practice. Hence, this chapter is devoted to some of the dynamic personalities in the communist movement from Karl Marx to Mao Tse-tung.

1. Karl Marx: Father of Modern Communism

Karl Marx has been called "The Man of the Century."[1] Yet his death was hardly noticed by the press and only about a dozen people attended his funeral. In a memorial address in Highgate Cemetery of London, Friedrich Engel, friend of Marx, declared: "The greatest living thinker will think no more . . . . Soon the world will feel the void left by the passing of the Titan. . . . His name and his work will live for centuries to come."[2]

In this century, Engels' prophecy has been fulfilled beyond his wildest dreams. Marx, being dead more than eighty years, "yet speaketh" with greater force than any prophet of this century. As Paul Tillich has observed, Marx's name have become so patently a political symbol that "whatever you say about him will be used against you by fanatics on both sides."[3]

Born in Trier, Prussia in the Rhineland of Germany, May 5, 1818, Marx came of a Jewish family and from a long line of rabbis, but his father, Hirschel, was a lawyer. In 1824, when Karl was six years old, his parents became Christians, perhaps more for political and economic considerations than convictions.

[1]*Time,* February 23, 1948.

[2]Karl Marx, *Selected Works.* New York: International Publishers, 1932, Vol. I, pp. 16-18.

[3]"How Much Truth Is There in Karl Marx?" *Christian Century,* September 8, 1948, p. 906.

At the University of Berlin, Marx came under the influence of the German philosopher, Georg Wilhelm Friedrich Hegel, leading thinker of the day, from whom he derived his dialectical method. From a critical student of Hegel, Ludwig Feuerbach, Marx got his materialistic view of all reality. Putting both conceptions together, Marx came up with his theory of dialectical materialism which will be discussed in more detail later.

Marx received his doctor's degree in 1841 at the University of Jena. His thesis dealt with a comparative study of the naturalism of Epicurus and Democritus. In 1843, Marx joined the radical news staff of the *Rheinische Zeitung* in Cologne and became the editor. The paper was immediately suppressed because of its socialistic message.

In 1844 Marx went to Paris to study socialism and met Friedrich Engels who was to become his intellectual mentor and financial supporter. Expelled from Paris in 1845, Marx went to Brussels, where he and Engels propagandized and worked with the Federation of the Just, which later became the Communist League.

At a congress of the Communist League in 1847, a confession of faith was requested to clarify the principles of "scientific communism." Marx and Engels produced the now famous *Communist Manifesto* published in February, 1848.

Eventualy Marx was driven from the continent to London where he died in 1883. During his 34 years of exile in London he was largely supported by Engels, whose father was a wealthy cotton spinner with factories in Manchester, England and Westphalia, Germany.

In London Marx spent his time in studying, writing, and organizing international communism. He spent hours upon hours in the famous British Museum, poring over great historical documents and gathering data. Few would have dreamed that he was destined to shape the character of the next century.

The private life of Marx is most interesting. He fell in love with Fraulein Jenny von Westphalen, a neighbor and the daughter of an official of the Prussian government. Marx wrote poetry to his girl friend who, whenever she read it "burst into tears of joy and melancholy." The following is a sample:

If we can but weld our souls together,
Then with contempt I shall fling my glove into the world's face;
Then I, the creator, shall stride through the wreckage!

In June, 1843, Marx and Jenny were married. Despite the long
years of poverty and hardship they remained devoted to each
other all of their married life. Marx lived parasitically upon other
people's labor—his wife's, friends', and especially Engels'. In a
letter to Engels, Marx admitted that he lived above his means
so that his daughters "may make connections and contacts which
will assure their future."[4]

Marx did earn a few dollars by writing a column for the *New
York Herald Tribune* (for $5.00 each) when he served for ten
years as a London correspondent. But, for the most part, he lived
off of the work of others. So far as can be determined, he was
arrested only once—for trying to pawn his wife's silver in a
pawn shop. But this was with the consent of Mrs. Marx; hence,
Karl was released.

Only three of Marx's children lived to maturity. When one
of his children died, he did not have enough money to buy a
coffin. Neighbors chipped in and purchased one. Only two
children survived him. Both of them, daughters, committed sui-
cide.

Two of the most significant books by Marx were his *Das
Kapital* or *Capital* and the *Communist Manifesto* written in collaboration with Engels. *Capital*, Vol. I, was published in 1867,
after eighteen years of work. This was Marx's *Magnum Opus*,
yet its sale did not even pay for the cheap cigars he smoked
while writing it. Upon completing the volume, Marx declared
it was "the task to which I have sacrificed my health, my happiness in life and my family."[5] Today *Capital* has become the
"Bible" of communism. Engels finished the other two volumes
after Marx's death.

[4]Cited by Dagobert Runes, *The Soviet Impact Upon Society*. New York:
Philosophical Library, 1953, p. 7.

[5]*Selected Correspondence 1846-1895, Karl Marx and Friederich Engels.*
Trans. by Dona Torr, in Marxist Library, Vol. XXIX. New York: International Press, 1942, p. 219.

The *Communist Manifesto*, published in 1848, has become the "creed" of the communists. It is the intellectual stimulus and inspiration of all communists, their modern "Sermon on the Mount." Many passages are in lyrical prose and few can read it without being emotionally stirred and intellectually stimulated. Hence the *Manifesto* must be read critically to discover the errors of Marx. But in spite of its errors, the *Manifesto* has become one of the most influential political documents in history.

It is impossible to estimate the influence of Marx on contemporary society. Suffice it to say that Marx belongs to that group of thinkers "who throw potent thought-foment into the world, and set in motion the masses of mankind."[6]

2. V. I. Lenin: Promoter of the Russian Revolution

Vladimir Ilyich Ulyanov alias N. Lenin was the man behind the communist revolution in Russia. A small bald-headed man with a goatee, Lenin was not an impressive figure. Joseph Stalin recorded his first impression of Lenin at his first meeting with him in 1905:

> I expected to see the mountain eagle of our Party a great man, not only politically but physically, for I had formed for myself a picture of Lenin as a giant, a fine figure of a man. What was my disappointment when I saw the most ordinary looking individual, below middle height, distinguished from ordinary mortals by nothing, literally nothing.[7]

But appearances are often deceptive, as Stalin was soon to discover in the case of Lenin. Lenin was brilliant, a fiery orator, and gifted with powers to persuade people to accept his views and to follow his leadership. His private life was characterized by order and discipline. He lived a simple life and was absolutely devoted to the communist cause, with little thought for himself. A good family man, Lenin liked to work at home rather than join the "bull sessions" in the cafes where Russian radicals gathered.

[6]M. Beer, *The Life and Teaching of Karl Marx.* Trans. by T. C. Partington and H. J. Stenning. New York: International Publishers, 1929, p. 7.

[7]*Stalin's Kampf*, edited by M. R. Werner. New York: Howell, Soskin & Co., 1940, p. 6.

Personally he was not a particularly vicious man, but did condone any method which promoted the revolution. For him, that which promoted the revolution was "good," that which prevented it "bad."

Born in Simbrisk on the Volga River in 1870, Lenin was the son of a provincial inspector and superintendent of schools with the honorific title of "Actual State Councillor." Hence, Lenin had the status of nobility. At the age of eighteen he had begun a serious study of Marxist literature. When his brother, Alexander, was executed for a plot against the life of Czar Alexander III, Lenin was moved to declare: "I'll make them pay for this! I swear it!"[8] His subsequent career was bent on carrying out this threat.

After practicing law in Samara, Lenin moved to St. Petersburg (1894) where he engaged in socialist propaganda. Exiled to Siberia for three years, he was joined by a young woman, Nadezhda Krupskaya, whom he had met in St. Petersburg. They were married and, upon release from banishment, went to Europe where Lenin published a revolutionary journal called *Iskra* (Spark) for circulation in Russia.

At the Second Congress of the Russian Social-Democratic Labor Party at London in 1903, the Party split into two factions: Bolsheviks (majority) and Mensheviks (minority). Lenin became the leader of the Bolsheviks, demanding that membership in the Party be a limited disciplined group, while the Mensheviks favored admitting everyone who supported the Party's general program. The future of the Communist Party was determined in this action. With a disciplined and dedicated group, the Bolsheviks overran all opposition to become the lords of Russia.

In 1905 Lenin returned from exile to Russia where he resumed revolutionary activities until 1907, when he again went abroad. For ten years he waited for the opportunity to re-enter Russia and to communize the country. Meantime Czar Nicholas was forced to abdicate on March 15, 1917. A Provisional Government under Prince Lvov and later Alexander Kerensky was established.

[8]David Shub, *Lenin*. New York: The New American Library of World Literature, 1950, p. 11.

Russia was at war with Germany. Troops were deserting the front and the people demanding bread and peace. Hence, the young government was harrassed by the Germans on the western front and the agitation of the Bolsheviks at home. Lenin's slogan that the "imperialist war be turned into a civil war" as a means of eliminating Russia as an enemy appealed to the German General Staff. Lenin was permitted, therefore, to travel in a "sealed" train through Germany. Arriving in St. Petersburg April 16, 1917, Lenin spurred the Bolsheviks (later called Communists) to step up their drive for peace.

Lenin's promises of "peace, bread and land," won over the workers and some of the military. On October 7, 1917, at 2:00 a.m. the revolution began with Leon Trotsky leading Lenin's forces. The Provisional Government fell and the Communist government set up. The first council of People's Commissars was organized with Lenin as chairman, Trotsky as head of Foreign Affairs, and Stalin as chairman of Affairs of Nationalities. Lenin then made peace with the Germans at Brest-Litovsk, and the first Communist constitution was adopted in 1918.

Under this constitution all lands, economic resources, factories, farms, and mines were confiscated by the government. Freedom of the press ended and the Cheka (secret police) was established to crush all opposition. Civil War engulfed Russia when volunteer armies fought against the communist regime. Terror and bloodshed were widespread.

Three years of communist rule brought Russia to the brink of economic chaos. Lenin was forced to provide a partial return to private enterprise and a free market. Called the New Economic Policy (NEP), this program made for improvement of economic conditions, but failed to provide political freedom.

Lenin's two chief contributions to communism were: (1) a highly disciplined party. In his hands the "Dictatorship of the Proletariat" became "the Dictatorship of the Party." His was a one-party government run by a disciplined and dedicated elite. At the meeting in London in 1903, Lenin won by a hair's breadth to limit membership in the Party. Elton Trueblood has observed that if Lenin had not won at that point, subsequent history may have been quite different. He concludes: "To this day the victories of militant communism are won, in every case, not by a majority, but by a highly disciplined, unyielding, and dedicated minority";[9] (2) In the area of tactics and strategy of revolution. Lenin held that violence is essential for the achievement of a communist society. Tactics in terms of zigzags, retreats, practical compromises were to be followed when they furthered the revolution.

Lenin died January 21, 1924, at Gorki near Moscow. His embalmed body was placed on permanent exhibition in a large tomb in Moscow's Red Square. But his spirit is kept alive by millions of portraits, statues, stories (some true, some apocryphal), and the publications of his writings surpass the publication of the Bible. Each day thousands of people stand four and five abreast in long lines to pass through the tomb for a view of his body. "Lenin is alive" and "Lenin is with us" are slogans one sees in the Soviet Union. The dead Lenin has become the god of the godless.

3. Joseph Stalin: Communist "Man of Steel"

Months before the death of Lenin, certain communist leaders engaged in a ruthless struggle to be his successor. Among these were Leon Trotsky and Joseph Vissarionovich Djugashvili, alias Joseph Stalin. Lenin declared: "Stalin is too rude, and this fault . . . becomes insupportable in the office of General Secretary."[10] He proposed that some way be found to get rid of Stalin on the grounds that he already had enormous power which he did not know how to use with sufficient caution. But Stalin outsmarted all of his rivals to become the supreme dictator of the Soviet Union.

Born in Gori, a town in the Caucasus, December 12, 1879, Stalin's father was a shoemaker. Three of his children had died due to poverty. About to bear her fourth child, his wife pledged it to the service of God. The child was called Joseph ("Soso" by his mother) after the Christian, Saint Joseph.

When Stalin was eleven, his father died. At the age of fourteen, Joseph entered the Tiflis Theological Seminary to study

[9]*The Yoke of Christ.* New York: Harper and Brothers, 1958, p. 114.
[10]Robert V. Daniels, editor, *A Documentary History of Communism.* New York: Random House, 1960, Vol. I, p. 225.

for the priesthood in the Greek Orthodox Church. Five years later (1899) he was expelled for rebelling against the stern rules of the Seminary and for reading revolutionary literature, including Marx's *Das Capital*. By this time he had already become a Marxist, having joined the Social Democratic Party in 1896.

When the Party divided into the Bolsheviks and Mensheviks in 1903 at London, Stalin sided with the former. Six times between 1902-1913 he was arrested for political activities and sent to Siberia, but always managed to escape. Imprisoned from 1913-17, he was freed in the revolution of February, 1917. He first met Lenin in 1905 at the Bolshevik Conference in Tammerfors, Finland. Thereafter he became a close associate of Lenin.

Stalin participated in the Bolshevik revolution October, 1917 when the Provisional Government was overthrown, and was appointed to the post of Minister of Nationalities as well as becoming a charter member of the Politburo of the new communist government. At the Eleventh Party Congress (March 27-April 2, 1922), with the nomination of Lenin, Stalin was elected to the office of General Secretary of the Party with Molotov as his assistant.

Stalin's chief enemy was Leon Trotsky who actually led the Bolsheviks to victory in the October Revolution and who had built up the great Red Army. He was the logical successor of Lenin. But when Lenin died, Trotsky was away from Moscow and Stalin purposely failed to inform him as to the exact date of the funeral. Hence, Stalin made all the funeral arrangements, calling attention to himself as the great friend of Lenin.

Stalin's personality and personal life are of importance to our understanding of communism's development in Russia. His alias, "Stalin," means "Man of Steel," a fitting name which reflects his personality, for steel is cold, hard, unfeeling. Such was his attitude toward others, even his own kin. There is little evidence that he loved his parents. He rarely wrote or saw his widowed mother. Upon the occasion of her death in 1937, he did send a wreath, but the event of her death went unmentioned in the Moscow press.

Stalin's first wife, Catherine, was a deeply religious person.

She bore him a son, Jacob, but she died of tuberculosis in 1907. At the funeral Stalin is reported to have remarked: "She is dead, and with her have died my last warm feelings for all human beings."[11] In 1918 at the age of 39, Stalin married his seventeen-year-old secretary, Nadiezhda, who bore him two children, a son Vasili and Svetlana, a daughter. At a party during the great famine in 1932, Mrs. Stalin expressed her sympathy for the starving people of Russia. Later at home there was a quarrel with her husband who resented her remarks about the starving populace. As a result, Mrs. Stalin went to bed and shot herself in the heart with a pistol. Or did Stalin do the deed? The truth may never be made known. The official announcement in the papers was that she had died during an emergency operation.

Those whom Stalin gathered around himself—factotums, lackeys, yes-men—were treated as slaves. After being summoned to his office, these people never knew whether they would go home or to jail. A man with insatiable thirst for power, Stalin sacrificed both family and friends to obtain it.

Stalin's 1929 slogan was "Liquidation of the Kulaks," farmers who owned land and who refused to give their farms to the state. When questioned by Sir Winston Churchill as to how many of these farmers were liquidated, Stalin replied: "Ten millions. It was fearful. Four years it lasted . . . It was very bad and difficult—but necessary."[12]

During the great purges of 1935-1939, many of the old Bolsheviks who helped to achieve the success of the revolution were accused of plotting to kill Stalin and were shot. Trotsky who was in exile was sentenced to the same fate. Some of the leading generals of the Red Army were shot on the trumped-up charges that they had violated their military oath and betrayed their country. An estimated 30,000 officers were purged from the army and navy. Trotsky was pursued to Mexico where he was murdered in 1940.

Even the artists who did not write or perform to suit Stalin were persecuted, browbeaten, or murdered. The great Shosta-

[11]Louis Fischer, *The Life and Death of Stalin*. New York: Harper and Brothers, 1952, p. 64.

[12]*The Hinge of Fate*. New York: Houghton Mifflin Co., 1950, p. 498.

kovich was repeatedly denounced because his music displeased
Stalin. To escape the wrath of Stalin, great writers such as
Boris Pasternak turned to translating and editing other writers
such as Puskin and Tolstoy whose works were not banned.

Stalin had a monstrous appetite for praise of himself. He saw
to it that history was rewritten to make him the hero of the
revolution. All official biographies set him up as a god to be
worshipped. Songs, poems, hymns, were sung with sickening
flattery to his name. The following hymn of praise is an example:

> O Great Stalin, O leader of the Peoples,
> Thou who dids't give birth to men,
> Thou who dids't rejuvenate the centuries,
> Thou who givest blossom to the spring,
> Thou who movest the chords of harmony,
> Thou splendid of my spring, O thou,
> Sun reflected in a million hearts.

Or take the following idolatrous "Song about the Returned Sun":

> We receive our sun from Stalin,
> We receive our prosperous life from Stalin . . .
> Even the good life in tundras filled with snow-storms
> We made together with him,
> With the Son of Lenin,
> With Stalin the Wise.[13]

Over the coffin of Lenin, Stalin swore to fulfill Lenin's program to communize the world. Couched in the style of the
homiletics learned at the Tiflis Thelogical Seminary, Stalin said
in part:

> In leaving us, Comrade Lenin ordered us to strengthen and ex-
> pand the Union of the Republics. We swear to Thee, Comrade
> Lenin, to honor Thy command.

> In leaving us, Comrade Lenin enjoined us to be faithful to the
> Communist International. We swear to Thee, Comrade Lenin,
> that we shall dedicate our lives to the enlargement and reinforce-

[13]Cited by Leon Trotsky, *Stalin*. New York: Grosset and Dunlap, 1941,
p. 394.

ment of the union of the workers of the whole world, the Communist International.[14]

These words should have been taken seriously by leaders of
the West negotiating with Stalin at Yalta, Teheran, and Potsdam.
Even at these meetings his post-war blueprint included the
conquest of the whole world.

Stalin had declared that all the Russians wanted to live in
peace with all other peoples of the world. In less than one
year after the close of World War II, it became clear to all
that Stalin was bent on keeping his pledge to his dead Comrade
Lenin. Stalin began to rewrite history, making it appear that
Russia had won the war amost single-handedly! This in spite
of the fact that the Western Allies, particularly the U.S.A., had
sent the Russians billions of dollars in aid. In return, Stalin
began to label the U.S. as a war mongering nation bent on the
destruction of the Soviet Union itself. To keep the Russian
people in fear and to build up the striking power of the Soviet
Union, Stalin trumped up the charge that the imperialistic
West was about to attack. At that very moment the Allies
were rapidly withdrawing troops from Europe.

Stalin so completely distorted Marxism that the "founding
father" would scarcely recognize it. He developed a new theory
of revolution—"Socialism in one country"—with a series of five-
year plans to achieve this goal. The Party became a centralized,
all-powerful bureaucracy. The classical theory of the "withering
away of the State" was abandoned; he condemned equalitaria-
nism as a "petit-bourgeois deviation" and a crime against the
State; he collectivized the farms with cruel coercion; he en-
couraged the growth of nationalism as against an international
outlook of communism; and he became the absolute dictator
with an imperialistic program which made the Czars look like
petty politicians.

On March 5, 1953, Stalin died, allegedly from a stroke—some
say murder. He rose from the status of a divinity student to
a "divine" dictator, from a priest of the church to the high
priest of communism. Stalin's body was placed beside Lenin's

[14]*Ibid.* pp. 382-383.

in the glass case in the marble mausoleum of Red Square where it remained until November, 1961, when Khrushchev ordered it removed and buried behind the walls of the Kremlin.

4. Nikita Khrushchev: "The New Look"

After the death of Stalin, Nikita Sergeyevich Khrushchev, by shrewd political maneuvering became the undisputed boss of the Soviet Union. A word is in order concerning his life, personality and policies.

Born April 17, 1894, in the village of Kalinovka, Kursk Region, Khrushchev's father was a coal miner. Nikita worked with his father as a mining machinery repair mechanic. He joined the Communist Party in 1919. Upon graduation from the Worker's Faculty (a school designed to train workers and peasants for higher schools) Khrushchev, in 1929 entered the Industrial Academy in Moscow which trained executives in the national economy of the USSR. By 1935, he had become First Secretary of the Moscow Regional and City Party Committees and in 1939 became a full member of the Political Bureau. He now holds both the premiership and the post of First Secretary of the Party to which he was elected September, 1953. In March, 1958, the Supreme Soviet of the USSR appointed Khrushchev Chairman of the Council of Ministers of the USSR. Thus he has become the undisputed and unchallenged head of the Soviet Government.

Khrushchev's path from the poverty-stricken village of Kalinovka to the Kremlin was a bloody one. For he climbed to the Kremlin pinnacle over a pile of corpses. As Stalin's hatchetman, he was directly responsible for the herding of millions of people into slave-labor camps and the shooting of thousands by the secret police.

As First Secretary of the Ukraine during the Great Purge of 1937-1939, he was responsible for the liquidation of untold thousands. In 1943 the German Army discovered ninety-five mass graves with nearly 10,000 bodies fully clothed, hands tied, and shot in the nape of the neck. Thousands more may lie in Ukranian graves never to be discovered. For when the Germans retreated, Khrushchev returned to the Ukraine to murder more people. Ukrainians in the free world declare that the post-war purge was more terrible than before the war.

In 1957 Khrushchev purged the so-called "anti-party" members of the Presidium—Malenkov, Molotov, Kaganovich, and Shepilov, and packed this organization with his lackeys. Kaganovich was the man who first took Khrushchev under his wing and helped him to rise to power.

The "Killer in the Kremlin" has a personality in sharp contrast to his predecessor, Stalin. A gregarious, loquacious, backslapping character, he enjoys the spotlight of the world. A dedicated communist, he uses every occasion and incident to denounce the capitalist West. Even his crude humor is directed at "decadent capitalism." In 1957 the author, with an American delegation, spent two and one half hours in Khrushchev's Kremlin office. In this group was a tall, thin student from one of our American colleges. Immediately upon shaking hands, Khrushchev exclaimed: "You are the skinniest-looking fellow I have ever seen to come out of a rich capitalist country! Don't they feed you over there? You are a disgrace! I'm going to keep you in the Soviet Union and fatten you up before you go back home."

In appearance Khrushchev is short, pudgy, bull-necked, and stands about five feet and four inches, weighing about two hundred pounds. He is bald wth the exception of a halo of white fuzz around his head. He is not a flabby man despite his weight and appears to be physically strong and to possess boundless energy.

Khrushchev's family is of interest. Nina, his wife, is a school teacher. They have three daughters—Julia, Rada, and Lena—and one son, Sergei. Their eldest son, a pilot, was killed in World War II. Also there are five grandchildren whom Khrushchev takes for walks when the opportunity permits.

His Kremlin office desk is cluttered with model planes, rockets, and mementos. In recent years, his doctors have put him on the water-wagon so far as hard liquors are concerned. He informed our delegation that he did not use tobacco in any form.

Among the new features of the "new look" in the USSR

initiated by Khrushchev are: (1) the decentralization of industry from a single center in Moscow to a system of Economic Councils operating in localities within the fifteen Republics; (2) a seven-year plan designed to surpass the capitalist West in the production of everything; (3) improvements in education, combining academic studies with vocational training; (4) encouragement of scientific developments; (5) more contact with other nations; (6) "peaceful coexistence"; and (7) at the 22nd Congress of the CPSU meeting in Moscow (1961), Khrushchev presented a plan to communize the whole world in twenty years.

By "peaceful coexistence," Khrushchev declares, that it is possible for countries with different social systems to live together in friendly competition without resorting to war. A close examination of his pronouncements on the doctrine reveals that it is nothing more than war under the label of "peace."[15] It is a high-sounding phrase which has nothing to do with the establishment of peace on earth and good will to men.

The notion that communists and the free world can coexist is a contradiction of what Marx, Lenin, and Stalin taught. Khrushchev knows this and engages in double-talk in dealing with this doctrine of peaceful coexistence. For example, at a Polish Communist Party meeting in Warsaw, (April, 1955) referring to the communist world and the West, he declared:

> We must realize that we cannot coexist eternally, for a long time. One of us must go to the grave. We do not want to go to the grave. They do not want to go to their grave either. So what can be done? We must push them to their grave.[16]

Freedom-loving nations must never forget that the communists have a *weltanschauung*, a world view, and that under the leadership of Khrushchev they are out to capture all peoples by any means at their disposal. Khrushchev is deadly serious when he declares: "We must push them [western nations] into their grave."

[15]See Harry and Bonaro Overstreet, *The War Called Peace*. New York: W. W. Norton, 1961.

[16]Quoted in *The Profile of Communism*. Prepared by the Anti-Defamation League of B'nai B'rith. New York: Freedom Books, 1961 p. vii.

5. *Mao Tse-tung: The Poet Dictator*

Red China's dictator, Mao Tse-tung (means "Hair Anoint East") arose from the status of a peasant to that of the leader of more than six-hundred million people. Born in the village of Shao Shan, Hunan Province, China, his father was a domineering peasant rice trader and his mother a docile, faithful Buddhist. Mao's mother hoped that he might enter the Buddhist priesthood. His father had plans for him to develop the family business. He refused to accept either plan for his future.

Mao attended the Changsha Middle School, in the capital of Hunan Province where he came into contact with Western ideas, graduating in 1918. After one year in the army, he took courses in Peking University (1918-1919). Here he met Li Ta-Chao, the librarian, who later became the real founder of the Communist Party in China. Also here at the university he discovered the writings of Marx and was converted to socialism. He then set about helping to organize communist movements in China.

In 1920 Mao married the daughter of one of the professors at Peking University. She was later executed (1928) by Ho Chien, general in Chiang Kai-shek's army. He divorced his second wife, who had gone to Moscow in the early years of the war between the Communists and the Nationalists.

In 1921 Mao was present at the meeting in Shanghai at which the Chinese Communist Party was founded. In 1922, Mao became secretary of the branch of the Communist Party of the Hunan Province and by 1923 he had become a member of the all-powerful Central Committee of the Party.

To aid him in building the Red army of China, Mao enlisted an able leader in Chu Teh. Both of these men became experts in planning and executing guerrilla warfare by which they were able to defeat large armies sent on "annihilation campaigns" against the communists by Nationalist leader Chiang Kai-shek.

By 1934, Mao's armies were surrounded by Nationalist troops, but they managed to escape and to stage a famous "Long March" of 6,000 miles from Kanhsien in South China to Yenan in Shensi Province in the northwest where Mao, as Chairman of the People's Republic of China, set up headquarters.

During World War II, Mao's communists joined with Chiang Kai-shek against the Japanese. But after the Allied victory of the United States, Britain, and France in 1945 over Japan, the communists made an all-out effort to take China. By late 1949, Mao and his men had driven Chiang's Nationalists off the mainland of China to the small island of Formosa.

Mao officially announced the formation of the communist government of China on October 1, 1949, as the "Chinese People's Republic" with himself as Chairman and Chou En-lai as premier. Peking was made the capital of the new communist regime. On February 4, 1950, at Moscow, Mao signed a thirty-year Sino-Soviet treaty of friendship and mutual defense.

Among Mao's literary achievements are numerous books which form the theoretical basis for the communists of China. Besides his writings in prose, he has gained recognition for his poetry. He is a master of classical verse, writing classical poetry with modern feeling and social content. A collection of about seventy of his poems have been brought together under the title *Wind Sand Poems,* which includes one long poem written in memory of his dead wife.

Today Mao is the undisputed dictator of Red China. Once in power, he eliminated all opposition by propaganda, terror, brain-washing, and military force. It has been estimated that 15 million people were murdered at his command and millions more imprisoned or enslaved in labor camps.

A man of great patience, military genius, author, poet, Mao now controls more people than any man on earth. At his command is a regular army of 2.5 million men, a navy, an air force, and 200 million militia men. Under his direction, China has already launched a nuclear energy program on a massive scale. At the present rate of advancement, Red China will become a serious threat to the peace of the whole world in the not too distant future.

CHAPTER III

Central Concepts of Communism

To understand communism in action, it is necessary to examine its theoretical doctrines and dogmas. While it is impossible to deal with the whole communist doctrinal frame of reference in this study, the basic elements can be described. Hence, the communist concepts of history, state, economics, man, morality, and religion are considered.

1. The Communist View of History

For centuries man has given serious thought to the meaning of history. Two major views have been held as to the nature and goal of the historical process. The Greeks, for example, viewed the whole time process as proceeding in endless cycles without arriving at any definite goal. The other view of history is moving upward toward a particular goal. Karl Marx held the latter notion and saw all history moving inevitably toward a social Utopia right here on earth.

Three fundamental factors are seen in the Marxian philosophy of history: dialectical materialism, historical materialism, and class struggle.

(1) Dialectical materialism. Marx thought he had discovered the key to history in dialectical materialism, that is, the conception of history as being dialectic, developing from one form of organization through conflict to the next higher stage by an inevitable self-determining progressive movement. Marx is indebted to philosopher Georg W. F. Hegel, for his concept of dialectical process. According to this theory there is a thesis, antithesis, and synthesis. The thesis affirms the proposition; the antithesis denies or negates it; and the synthesis embraces what is true in both the thesis and the antithesis, and this brings the movement one step nearer to reality.

Marx applied the dialectic to economics. For example, there

is the thesis called Capitalism, the antithesis is the contradictions within Capitalism, and the synthesis is Socialism. Or to put it on a broader scale, a thesis could be primitive Communism, the antithesis Capitalism, and the synthesis Communism.

Since Hegel applied the dialectic only to ideas and not to the material, Marx claimed that he found him standing on his head and therefore put him on his feet.[1] Instead of applying the dialectic to ideas, Marx applied it to history and economics. To put it another way, Marx played the dialectic idealistic music of Hegel in a materialistic key.

From Ludwig Feuerbach, philosopher and pupil of Hegel, Marx discovered that all reality is materialistic in nature. He accepted Feuerbach's view that religion is a mere reflection of man's material conditions. Indeed, Marx, with Feuerbach, saw all thought, philosophy, and society as derivatives of the material conditions of man.

(2) Historical materialism. The dialectical philosophy borrowed from Hegel was transformed by Marx into dialectical materialism from which in turn historical materialism derives. In other words, historical materialism, the materialist interpretation of history, is dialectical materialism applied primarily to economics. Thus social change is to be sought not in ideas or ideals, but in the modes of production and exchange. His fundamental proposition is summed up by his lifelong friend and supporter, Friedrich Engels. The proposition is:

> . . . that in every historical epoch, the prevailing mode of economic production and exchange, the social organization necessarily following from it, form the basis upon which is built up, and from which alone can be explained, the political intellectual history of that epoch; that consequently the whole history of mankind (since the dissolution of primitive tribal society, holding land in common ownership) has been a history of class struggles, contests between the exploiting and the exploited, ruling and oppressed classes; that the history of these class struggles forms a series of evolution in which, now-a-days, a stage has been reached where the exploited and the oppressed class—the prole-

[1]*Capital.* New York: The Modern Library, n.d., "Author's Prefaces," p. 25.

tariat—cannot attain its emancipation from the sway of the exploiting and ruling classes—the bourgeoisie—without, at the same time, and once and for all, emancipating society at large from all exploitation, oppression, class distinctions, and class struggles.[2]

Thus when the "productive forces" (instruments of production as labor and practical skill) change, there comes about a change in "productive relations" (relations between men).

As Marx saw it, the dialectical process runs through the whole structure of things. It gives rise to economic determinism and an interpretation of history which develops through a series of stages. It begins with the period of primitive communism. This was a simple, undifferentiated society in which everybody owned the simple tools of production and lived a communal life. There was no private property, no class divisions, and no state.

This simple primitive society broke down with the introduction of division of labor and private property, and hence the division of people into classes. Out of this situation arose a slave-holding society with the owner possessing the means of production. It was a society characterized by a master-slave relationship.

The next stage of economic history was brought about by a change in the means of production and was called the feudal economy. At this stage the new productive forces caused a change in social relations. The production system became more complicated. Greater initiative was needed on the part of the workers, and so slavery was modified to serfdom. Developing industry and commerce required that the workers have more initiative and greater skills. Under this system, men were not owned directly by the landlord but had to give him free work in order to till the land.

With the coming of the industrial revolution and its new means of production, another economic order arose, namely, capitalism. The merchant class overthrew the feudal lords and set up the capitalistic society. Factories arose with a more complicated system of production which in turn brought about a change in human relations. The means of production were in

[2]Engels' Preface to the Communist Manifesto of 1848.

Steps in the Marxist theory of history:

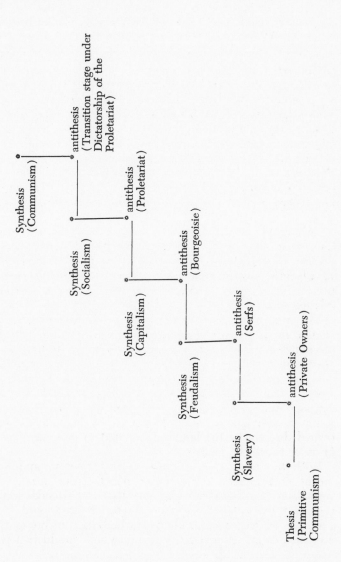

the hands of a few capitalists and the wage earners worked for
them. The capitalists paid back to the worker only a small
portion which he had produced and kept for himself the remains.
This, Marx called "Surplus Value" which rightly belonged to
the workers.

The next stage of economic development is that of socialism
in which the means of production are owned by the state. It is
a period of transition between the capitalist and communist
systems of society. In other words, it is the period of the
revolutionary transformation of capitalism to communism. During
this period, society is to be ruled by "dictatorship of the
proletariat" or the dictatorship of the working class over the
defeated capitalists and exploiters.

The final stage of economic development is that of communism in which capitalism will have disappeared, the classless
society established, the state "withered away," and every man
living according to the principle, "from every man according to
his ability and to every man according to his need." Thus
communism will provide a perfect society of brotherhood and
justice.

(3) Class struggle. In the *Communist Manifesto*, Marx declared: "The history of all hitherto existing society is the history
of class struggles." According to him, the dynamic of the dialectical process is class struggle which keeps pushing history
toward its ultimate goal of a classless society. Thus when the
classless society is achieved, class struggle will cease because
there will no longer be a tension between "the haves" and
"the have nots." Everything will be owned by the people.
National differences will disappear for "the working class has
no country." Consequently, wars will pass along with class
struggles and the state. History will then have arrived at the
goal of complete perfection and the dialectical process will no
longer prevail since the classless society has arrived. In this
paradisaical and utopian society, man will live happily and
peacefully in co-operative fellowship with his fellowman. This
is the eschatology of communism and it has a profound appeal
to the masses of underprivileged peoples. It is the belief in
the kingdom of this world. Communists hold that history is

inevitably moving in the direction of this social utopia and that the forces of the universe are on their side.

2. *Theory of Economics*

At the graveside of Karl Marx, Engels said: "The materialist interpretation of history and the theory of surplus value are Marx's great discoveries." The core of the whole economic theory of Marx is that of "surplus value." He claims that the whole capitalistic system depends upon the production of surplus value.

Ironically, Marx's economic theory is derived from the classical economists of England. Adam Smith in his *Wealth of Nations* ("the Bible of capitalism"), has argued that "Labour is the real measure of the exchangeable value of all commodities."[3] Marx took his cue from this idea and reasoned that if the whole value of a commodity was due to the labor which had gone into it, why should it not be paid to the man who produced it? He thus modified the labor theory of his contemporaries. Smith had argued that "the value which the workers add to their materials resolves itself into two parts of which one pays their wages and the other is the profit of the employer." Marx called the second part "surplus value" which the capitalist appropriates for himself, but rightly belongs to the worker.

Marx, therefore, concluded that the measure of value is labor-time (the measure of exchange value), but the laborer gets barely enough to live on. Capital, therefore is unpaid labor.[4]

Labor possesses, then, the unique quality of being able to produce more than is required for subsistence and replacement. The worker receives only a sufficient amount to keep him alive and going. For example, a man works 12 hours and in the first 6 of these he produces all the value he is to receive as wages. Of the value produced in the second 6 hours, he gets nothing. The first 6 hours of labor Marx calls "necessary labour-time" and the labor expended during that time "necessary labour." During the second 6 hours, the worker creates a surplus-value

[3]New York: The Modern Library, 1937, p. 30.
[4]*Capital, op. cit.*, p. 585.

which goes into the hands of the capitalist. This he calls "surplus labour-time," and "surplus-labour." And Marx held that all produced in this period should go to the worker also.[5]

Marx concludes that all commodities as values are only definite means of "congealed labour-time."[6] Therefore, a useful article has a value only because human labor in the abstract has been embodied or materialized in it.[7]

This doctrine of "surplus value" which was supposed to demonstrate the exploitation of wage earners was arrived at by Marx by applying labor-time value to wages, but not to the prices of manufactured articles. Obviously the production of some goods require less labor and are greater in value than certain products which demand more hours of work.

From his theory of surplus value, Marx derived his famous three laws of capitalism. First there is the Law of Capitalist Accumulation.[8] According to this law, capitalists are forced by competition to accumulate more capital in terms of labor-saving devices to produce more goods. This in turn results in a drop in profits. The second law is that of Concentration of Capital.[9] As a result of competition, the number of capitalists become smaller for the weaker ones are driven from the field to swell the ranks of the wage earners. Hence there is created an "industrial reserve army." In other words, "one capitalist kills another." In order to survive, capitalism inevitably leads to monopoly in the form of trusts and cartels, for it is in this way that they become strong enough to withstand recurrent economic crises. The third law is that of Increasing Misery.[10] According to this law, capitalists are forced to compensate for the decline of their profits by intensifying their exploitation of the worker. Hence more hours of unpaid labor are demanded. The burgeoning "industrial reserve army" enables him to still further reduce wages.

[5]*Ibid.*, pp. 240-41.
[6]*Ibid.*, p. 46.
[7]*Ibid.*, p. 45.
[8]*Ibid.*, p. 671ff.
[9]*Ibid.*, p. 681ff.
[10]*Ibid.*, p. 708ff.

Marx saw capitalism as a leech that lives on the lifeblood of the worker. Since he believed that capitalism could not be reformed, he advocated that it must be destroyed. And revolution is necessary to accomplish this. To get rid of capitalism and private property, Marx advocated expropriation, the transference of ownership of property from individuals to the state.

3. The Communist View of the State

According to Marx, the State is not a natural order or a divine institution, but an historic outgrowth of society. It is a result of conquest by a dominant class, namely the bourgeoisie. In the hands of the ruling class the State is an organ of oppression of the ruled. Hence, Marx defined the State as "the executive committee" of the bourgeoisie.[11]

The State, then, is the form of organization adopted by the owners to protect their private property and interests. Therefore, the State, as Marx sees it, is a machine for repression of the working class.[12] Thus the State is to be captured and destroyed. Marx amended the *Communist Manifesto* of 1872 to read: "The proletariat must smash the existing state machine."

Between the abolition of the bourgeois State and the establishment of communist society lies the transition stage called "the dictatorship of the proletariat." This means that during this phase the State will still be coercive, but with the difference that the coercion will be exercised by the proletariat majority against the bourgeoisie minority. This is the period in which the workers take over the means of production, the State, and have armed forces to insure law and order.

But since the State arose out of classes it will disappear in a classless society. It will "wither away."[13] For a while after the revolution people will still behave in terms of the old order, but they will become adjusted to the new life and repressive measures will no longer be needed, hence, no State. For when

[11]*Communist Manifesto.* Chicago: Henry Regnery Co., 1954, p. 18.

[12]Karl Marx and Friedrich Engels, *The German Ideology.* New York: International Publishers, 1947, p. 59.

[13]V. I. Lenin, "State and Revolution," *Selected Works,* 1943, Vol. VII, p. 24.

men become assured of a living, they will lose their greed and other evils which necessitate police force. Then the only function of the State will be administrative activities.

Marx does not describe in detail the withering away of the State nor just how far the withering process will go. But in the higher phase of communist society there will be no coercive State and society will inscribe on its banners: "From each according to his ability and to each according to his need."

4. The Marxist View of Man

"What is man?" is an age old question. Marx has a simple answer. Man is in his human essence "the ensemble of social relations."[14] That is to say, man is made by his environment in general and economic factors in particular.

As a believer in evolution Marx saw men as an historical series of beings which had developed in the beginning from mere tree-climbing ancestors. In Engels' essay, "The Part Played by Labor in the Transition from Ape to Man," he describes how human society arose out of a band of tree climbing monkeys.[15]

This whole theory of man's descent from animals is dramatically illustrated in the Lenin Museum of Natural History in Moscow. The first display from the Red Square entrance shows man's development from lower forms of life through monkeys, apes, to man.

What, then, actually distinguishes man from animals in Marxian thought? Man is a producing animal. Animals merely *use* nature; man *masters* it. Adopting Benjamin Franklin's famous definition of man as "a tool-making animal," the communists declare that this is what makes the difference between a man and an animal. Thus man has no metaphysical or religious basis. He is purely material, a part of nature. Even his mind is simply the highest product of matter. Mind, therefore, is merely the reflection of the material.

Marx spoke of individuals only insofar as they are personifi-

[14]*Theses on Feuerbach*, No. VI.

[15]*Dialectics of Nature*. New York: International Publishers, 1940, Chapter 9.

cations of economic categories and representatives of special classes of relations and interests. Hence a person has no absolute value. His value is seen only in relation to the collective society. Personality, therefore, is a function of class and the class a function of the dialectical process.

Basic to Marx's doctrine of man is that of self-estrangement or disunity. Something has come into man which splits his unity. Here Marx uses the Biblical imagery of the Fall of Man. This disunity appeared not because man wanted to be God, but was due to the rise of private property with its attendant exploitation. It was not due to sin, but because the producer was no longer the consumer. This came about by division of labor in which production became differentiated into occupations and man sold his produce to another man. The estrangement of man reached its climax in the capitalistic system, for the many became dependent on the few and the worker did not get what he produced.

What is man's salvation from disunity? How can he be saved from his dividedness? By the socialization of all capital. And when private property is eliminated and the producer consumes the goods he produces. When the worker becomes the ruler and there is no one to exploit him. In the classless society man will no more be estranged from himself. He will be at harmony with himself and all other men. He will be happy living in a peaceful paradise of a communist society.

5. The Marxist View of Morality

Does communism have an ethic? Some scholars say no and point to the *Communist Manifesto* which contains no word of "right" or "justice" and no appeal to any moral law. Lenin gives a positive answer to this question. He states emphatically that there is a communist morality. He describes it as follows:

> Often it is made to appear that we have no ethics of our own; and very often the bourgeoisie accuse us Communists of repudiating all ethics. This is a method of throwing dust in the eyes of the workers and peasants. In what sense do we repudiate ethics and morality? In the sense that it is preached by the

bourgeoisie, who declare that ethics were from God's command-ments.[16]

What is the nature of the communist ethic? What do the communists say about morality? In the first place, it is an ethic without transcendental reference. Engels declared: "We reject every attempt to impose on us any moral dogma whatsoever as an eternal, ultimate and forever immutable moral law. . . . We maintain . . . that all former moral theories are the product, in the last analysis, of the economic stage which society had reached at that particular epoch."[17]

Likewise Marx and Lenin denied any religious basis for human action. "Right can never be higher," says Marx, "than the eco-nomic structure of a society, and the cultural development thereby determined."[18] And Lenin declared, "morality taken from outside human society does not exist for us; it is a fraud."[19] Marx violently denounced all Christian ethical principles because they are grounded in God and allegedly unjust. In his words:

> The social principles of Christianity have now had eighteen hundred years to develop, and need no further development by Prussian consistorial councilors.

> The social principles of Christianity justified the slavery of an-tiquity, glorified the serfdom of the Middle Ages, and equally know, when necessary, how to defend the oppression of the proletariat, although they make a pitfall face over it.

> The social principles of Christianity preach the necessity of a ruling and an oppressed class, and all they have for the latter is the pious wish the former will be charitable.

> The social principles of Christianity transfer the consistorial coun-cilors' adjustment of all infamies to heaven, and thus justify the further existence of those infamies on earth.

[16]Address to the Third Congress of the Russian Young Communist League of October 20, 1920, "Tasks of the Youth Leagues," *Selected Works*, Vol. IX, p. 4-475.

[17]*Anti-Duhring*, Marxist Library, Vol. XVIII. New York: International Publishers, n.d., p. 109.

[18]"Critique of the Gotha Programme," *Selected Works*, 1933 Vol. II, p. 565.

[19]*Religion*. New York: International Publishers, 1933, p. 48.

The social principles of Christianity declare all vile acts of the oppressors against the oppressed to be either the just punishment of original sin and other sins or trials that the Lord in his infinite wisdom imposes on those redeemed.

The social principles of Christianity preach cowardice, self-contempt, abasement, submission, humility, in a word all the qualities of the *canaille*; and the proletariat, not wishing to be treated as *canaille*, needs its courage, its self-esteem, its pride, and its sense of independence more than its bread.

The social principles of Christianity are cringing, but the proletariat is revolutionary.

So much for the social principles of Christianity.[20]

In the second place the communist ethic is a class ethic. According to the communists, all ethical systems simply reflect the interests of the dominant class. Thus the communist class, or any class, generates an ethic of its own. Lenin declared: "Our morality is entirely subordinated to the interests of the class struggle of the proletariat. . . . We say: Morality is that which serves to destroy the old exploiting society and to unite all the toilers around the proletariat, which is creating a new communist society—we do not believe in an eternal morality."[21]

Again, the communist ethic is relativistic. The moral code is the product of particular social need. Change in the social need necessitates change in the moral code. Hence, there is no absolute moral value in Marxism. Right is relative to time, class, and the social goal.

In the fourth place, the communist ethic is an ethic of hate. Bertrand Russell, noted English philosopher, states that one of the primary reasons he is not a communist is that Marx was "almost entirely inspired by hatred"[22] Marxism satisfies impulses toward hatred and aggression toward others. The enemy

[20]"The Communism of the Paper *Rheinischer Beobachter*," Lewis S. Feuer, ed., *Marx and Engels: Basic Writing on Politics and Philosophy.* New York: Doubleday and Co., 1959, pp. 268-269.

[21]Address to the Third Congress of the Russian Young Communist League, *op. cit.*, p. 475, 477.

[22]"Why I Am Not A Communist," *Look*, April 30, 1957, p. 103.

must be destroyed and the capitalist system obliterated. Thus, hatred is generated in the masses toward the burgeoisie with the view to violently overthrowing them.

Again, the communist ethic is one which dehumanizes and depersonalizes the individual. The individual, apart from communism, has no value. A person who opposes the communist strategy must be liquidated. And he who conforms is stripped of all of his dignity, rights, and freedom.

And finally, the communist ethic is an ethic of the "end justifies the means." Hence the communists can resort to murder, slavery, "zig-zag" policy, and deception to achieve their goals. All of these tactics are justified if they promote the revolution. In short, that is right conduct which promotes revolution and wrong which prevents it. And in spite of brutal and inhumane methods, Khrushchev declares that communists "are guided by the most humane considerations in relations between human beings."[23]

Admittedly the communists lay great stress upon brotherhood and justice. But these are smoke screens to attract the naive and uncritical. It is these moral pretensions which make communism so evil and demonic. Yet one of the great appeals of communism is that it has become falsely identified as a high moral movement in our time professing to eliminate poverty, ignorance, and stand for peace and justice among all men.

6. Communism and Religion

In one striking sentence, Karl Marx summed up the communist view of religion by calling it "the opium of the people."[24] Echoing Marx, Lenin said that religion is "a kind of spiritual gin in which slaves of capital drown their human shape and their claims to any decent human life."[25] For Marx and Lenin and all communists, religion is illusory happiness of people and must be abolished for their real happiness. All religion is false and con-

[23]Interview with James Reston of *The New York Times*, October 7, 1957.

[24]"Toward the Critique of Hegel's Philosophy of Right," in Lewis S. Feuer, ed., *Marx and Engels: Basic Writings on Politics and Philosophy*, p. 263.

[25]"Socialism and Religion," *Selected Works*, 1943, Vol. XI, p. 658.

trary to true science. It is a tool of reaction, and an opiate of the people to calm the desires of the exploited for justice and to ease the consciences of the exploiters.

Atheism is a natural and inseparable element of communism. The writings of the "founding fathers," Marx, Engels, and Lenin are filled with virulent attacks upon God and religion. Marx held that man created God out of his own image and that religious sentiment itself is a social product. Lenin declared that "fear created a God," fear of the blind forces of capital, the taproot of all modern religion. Speaking for all communists Lenin declared, "We do not believe in God—we know perfectly well that the clergy, the landlords and bourgeoisie spoke in the name of God in order to pursue their exploiters' interest."[26]

Today Khrushchev has made it clear that he does not hold any belief in God. In an interview with Serge Groussand of the French newspaper, Le Figaro, March 19, 1958, Khrushchev asserted: "I think there is no God. I freed myself long ago from such a concept."[27] As did his predecessors, Khrushchev is now doing everything possible to eliminate the bewitching power of the opium of religion. He is an obedient disciple of Lenin who as early as 1909 declared that communists must use every practical method possible to eliminate the "social roots of religion."[28]

One cannot be a believer and a member of the Communist Party whose aim it is to stamp out the last vestige of belief in God. Hence, school teachers in the USSR are urged to be atheists and to be active fighters for antheism of the children. Thus a child is taught that all religion is superstition and unscientific. He is told that religion is a refuge of the weak and that only superstitious people hold to religious convictions.

Communism itself has become a secular faith. It seeks to supplant Christianity by claiming to have all the answers to the spiritual questions of the soul and to provide the real meaning of life.

[26]Op. cit. Address to the Third Congress of the Russian Young Communist League of October 2, 1920, p. 475.

[27]Cited in Soviet World Outlook, Department of State Publication 6838, Washington, D. C., July, 1959, p. 78.

[28]"Attitude of Worker's Party Toward Religion," Selected Works, 1943 Vol. XI, p. 666.

CHAPTER IV

The Case for Communism

Some would condemn communism as being wholly evil and without any merit. But a movement which has made such incredible gains in the past forty-five years cannot be written off as totally bad. It has certain values and achievements to its credit which free men must face realistically. Therefore, a strong case can be made for communism as well as against it. Rarely do American writers record any of these values, perhaps for fear of being misunderstood, misinterpreted, or being branded as communist sympathizers or dupes. But any fair and objective treatment of communism must acknowledge its achievements. We must examine, therefore, the case for as well as the case against this world movement.

In preparing a brief for communism, several factors must be taken into account. On the positive side of the ledger there are some items which have actually contributed at least indirectly to the strengthening of the free world.

Soviet communism has rendered democratic countries a genuine service by challenging them to reassess their purpose and potential. (One can usually get support for his pet project, if he points out that the communists are outdoing us in this or that particular field.) As a result of the communist challenge, we are attempting to build a better system of education, to strengthen our economic, political, and military potentials, and even to improve our morals! Hence, to a degree the Russians have stirred us to re-examine ourselves and to strengthen our own cause.

Arnold J. Toynbee has said that he does not believe that the Russians will succeed in imposing their way of life on America, rather they will cause us to develop and to improve our way of life. He illustrates what he means by telling the story of those fishermen from the North Sea Fleet who have difficulty in keeping their fish fresh. When the fish are caught they are placed in tanks, and before the fishermen get back home, the fish are often stale. But there was one captain of a trawler who brought back beautiful fish. They were quite different from all of the others, fresh and lively. The fisherman gave the explanation as follows: "You see, for every thousand live herring I put into my tank on my trawler, I put in one catfish. Now the catfish may eat one or two of the herring while on the way home, but he keeps the rest moving! He keeps them lively and they come back in beautiful condition."

Toynbee explains that communism is the catfish in the Western herring pond, and that, if we play our cards rightly and have the patience to play them wisely and sensibly, the unintended service that communism may do for us is to make us do many things in our own world which we might never have done at all by ourselves, if the communists had not been there to act the catfish to keep us lively and on the move.[1]

More specifically, communism has forced a bourgeois capitalist civilization to see more clearly its contributions and weaknesses. Marxists have criticized capitalism's tendency to be dominated by the selfish profit motive which resulted in the concentration of wealth in the hands of a few and widespread poverty among the masses. Its tendency to periodic cycles of prosperity and depression has also been a point of attack by the communists. Capitalism's response in the United States has been to adjust to the new age. The rise of trade unionism, enactment of state legislation, the awakening of the social consciousness within the capitalistic group itself, and the appearance of rapid technical change in productive industry have all served to modify capitalism in this country. As a result we now have a "welfare capitalism" which is quite different from the old laissez-faire capitalism which Marx confronted in Europe and England. It is a more balanced economy, a "mixed economy," though still predominantly capitalistic.

Thus Marx threw the spotlight on the economic ills of the nineteenth century culture characterized by man's inhumanity to man. His solutions to the economic problem must be rejected

[1]From a pamphlet entitled, "Russian Catfish and Western Herring," reprinted by permission of the *New York Herald Tribune*, by Oxford University Press, New York, n.d.

but his critique cannot be brushed aside as being invalid. And though present day communism still criticizes capitalism in nineteenth-century Marxist terms, which are no longer relevant as they once were, this criticism serves as a stimulus continually to improve our economic system.

Communism offers a vision of a transformed world. Its world view demands a society in which there is peace and plenty for everyone. Such a view provides an irresistible appeal to millions of people. "Where there is no vision, the people perish" (Proverbs 29:18). Marx declared: "The philosophers have only *interpreted* the world, in various ways; the point is to *change* it." (*Theses on Feuerbach,* No. XI.)

The vision of a better world has a particular appeal to this fragmented and frustrated generation. Berdyaev, the Russian philosopher, has pointedly said in this connection, "The whole world is burning, thirsting for transformation, seeking a new and better life. The strength of communism lies in its having a complete design for reconstructing the world's life, in which theory and practice, thought and will are one."[2] The visitor to the USSR is struck by the optimism of the youth who feel that they are building a new world. One high school student informed the writer that the youth of Russia desire to be builders of a new world while the youth of America want to be movie stars and cowboys! Tiran Nersoyan has well noted that Soviet achievements "have filled the intelligent youth and the masses alike of the USSR with enthusiasm and vision."[3]

It may be true that the communists are building a new Tower of Babel, but their collective goal brings a sense of fulfillment to the masses as they gear their energies to an ideal which sustains and stimulates them to action. Every individual is called to build a new world collectively.

In our own country we have lost the vision of the founding fathers of a great commonwealth, "the kingdom of God in America." Our general goal for society has become vague and has lost

[2]*The Russian Revolution.* Ann Arbor, Michigan: University of Michigan Press, 1961, p. 75.

[3]*The Christian Approach to Communism.* London: Frederick Muller, 1942, p. 8.

its dynamic. Arnold J. Toynbee, the historian, claims that America, with its "Madison Avenue" persuaders and its "handicap of affluence" have turned the United States from an "arch-revolutionary" power into an "arch-conservative" power. She began with a revolutionary spirit after the Declaration of Independence, but now, according to Toynbee, America has relinquished her revolutionary role to Russia.[4]

Toynbee further observes that the impetus behind the American Revolution was the spirit of Christianity which has now lost its thrust and power in America. It is his conviction that America launched the World Revolution by firing the shot heard around the world and that she can still rejoin the revolution. America must recover her vision and sense of destiny.[5]

The exponents of communism give voice to attractive ideals which have a profound appeal to millions. With its pretension of being a movement of moral excellence, communism has impressed the masses as well as some intellectuals as standing for righteousness, justice, equality, and peace. Joseph Stalin, himself, even declared that the value of the individual is the keynote of Soviet society! Emphasis on these ideals has lured many an intellectual into the communist camp, hoping to find an outlet for his social passion.[6]

Communism is a reminder to all Christians of an unfulfilled task, the lack of achievement of the Christian ideal of justice which has not worked itself out in society. As Berdyaev has observed, the Christian good has become too conventional and rhetorical, and so the carrying out of certain elements of that "good" which is proclaimed in theory but very inadequately achieved in practice, is undertaken in a spirit of terrible reaction against Christianity.[7]

Again, Marx saw the need for free education for all children in public schools and the abolition of child labor in factories.[8]

[4]*America and World Revolution.* New York: Oxford University Press, 1962.
[5]*Ibid.*
[6]See Richard Crossman, ed., *The God That Failed.* New York: Bantam Books, 1951.
[7]*Op. cit.*, p. 50.
[8]*The Communist Manifesto.*

The Soviets have developed a remarkable public school system for children seven to seventeen. The courses of study are rigorous with heavy emphasis upon science and technology combined with practical training in industrial and agricultural production.

Communism has made for incredible scientific and educational development in the Soviets. We have been misled by the assumption that Russia is a wholly "backward" country. True, it is "backward" in living standards and political organization. But in the area of scientific development and achievement, Russia has outstripped other nations to become the second greatest power in the world. Her achievements in this respect have come as a shock to the West, and have punctured our illusion that great industrial and scientific advances cannot occur under a totalitarian system.

Marx and the communists have made us aware of the central role that economics plays in our lives and in history. While we cannot accept Marx's dialectical materialism or economic interpretation of history, we must admit the fact that historians have largely ignored the economic factor until recent times. Marx's discovery of the simple fact that man must eat and drink and have clothes to wear is an elementary but basic one. Yet economic history is a recent development in historical studies. While man is more than an animal who eats and drinks, eighteenth century historians almost forgot the fact that while "man shall not live by bread alone," he must have bread.

Marx and the communists have succeeded in engendering a sense of guilt in the western world.[9] Certain people of wealth and fame have felt that it was not right to enjoy the good things of life while over half of the world went to bed hungry every night. Andre Gide, the noted French author, has stated that it was not Marxist theory that brought him to communism, but that the privileged position which he personally enjoyed seemed to be preposterous and intolerable in the midst of a needy world. He tells how this conviction came home to him:

> I once had occasion to talk with one of the shipwrecked survivors of *La Bourgogne* and he told me that he had been lucky

[9]Stephen Neill, *Christian Faith and Other Faiths*. London: Oxford University Press, 1961, pp. 164-68.

enough to get into a lifeboat in which a number of men had got away; if more had been taken in, the boat would have capsized and sunk. The men in safety on board, armed with jack-knives and hatchets, had hacked off the hands of those who, clinging to the sides of the boat, were endeavoring to scramble in out of the sea. The knowledge of being one of those in the lifeboat, of being safe, whilst others round me are drowning, that feeling became intolerable to me. People argue with me but I am not sufficiently expert to answer them subtly. I only cling tenaciously to the one fact that I cannot accept the place in a lifeboat in which only a limited number of people are saved. If I could feel, at least, assured that it was the best who were saved, it might not be so bad, but what makes me most indignant is when somebody says to me, "What are you grumbling at? You must admit that it is very comfortable in the lifeboat."[10]

Thus Gide became ashamed of being a man of independent means, of not being obliged to work with his own hands, of never having been forced to earn his living by the sweat of his brow. Communism appeared to be an answer to his need.

Communism has also engendered a sense of guilt in the churches which have often sided with those in power against the weak. Marx himself pointed out that Christianity justified slavery, that the churches of the Middle Ages were patterned after Feudal society sanctioning serfdom with church officials themselves in the role of Feudal lords, and that the church of the eighteenth century sided with the capitalist powers rather than with the working class.[11]

And in the America of the nineteenth century, the churches were practically out of touch with economic development. With the exception of the "social gospel" leaders from 1865 to 1915, the evils of capitalism went largely unchallenged by the churches. So it is not without reason that the churches have a guilty con-

[10]Richard Crossman, ed., *The God That Failed*. New York: Bantam Books, 1951, pp. 170-171.

[11]"Toward a Critique of Hegel's Philosophy of Right," in Lewis S. Feuer, ed., *Marx and Engels: Basic Writings on Politics and Philosophy*, p. 268.

science, particularly in their tendency to hold to a place of privilege and to ignore the underprivileged.

Finally, Marxism's eschatology presents a powerful appeal to the masses. Communism claims to be the "wave of the future." Coupled with the astounding success of communism in recent years, the promise of a "utopia tomorrow" finds a ready response among those who see no hope of escape from intolerable and unjust systems of economic oppression. When asked why the people of the Soviet Union were satisfied with such a small share in the vast industrial and agricultural production of their country, the writer was told that they were willing to sacrifice now so that their children could enjoy the abundant life promised by the communists in the next few decades. Khrushchev has already promised the people that in the next decade the USSR will have the highest standard of living in the world. It is the old donkey and carrot technique to lure the people forward in their work for the promised land that will flow with "milk and honey" for everyone.

CHAPTER V

The Case against Communism

Any criticism of Marxism logically begins with the theoretical presuppositions which underlie the communist movement. Thus, this section presents a critique of the roots as well as the fruits —strategies, tactics, results—of communism. An attempt will be made to evaluate Marxism in the light of historical and economic facts.

1. Marxist Philosophical Theory

The communist theory of history is based upon dialectical materialism, a contradiction in terms for there can be only a dialectic of reason and consciousness. Dialectics can exist only in mind and not in matter. The fact that modern Marxists are forced to admit the influence of mental life from material processes clearly indicates that dialectical materialism is "in reality not materialism at all."[1]

Marxists have never been able to demonstrate how matter is transformed into mental processes. Nor have they been able to work out the inter-relationship between the substructure (the world of matter) and the super-structure (the world of men's ideas, philosophy, religion, etc.). They declare that the latter is simply a reflection of the material. If this idea is applied to Marxism itself, it has no more validity than that of the bourgeois philosophy. For the Marxists claim that all philosophies are merely reflexes of the bourgeois mind, and if this is true, their philosophy is only a reflex of the proletarian mind and in no sense absolute. As V. C. Jeffreys observes: "Subjected to Marxist methods the whole Marxist ideology would appear as an elaborate and impressive rationalization of the psychology of the underdog."[2]

[1]N. O. Looskii, *History of Marxist Philosophy.* New York: International University Press, 1951, p. 364.

[2]*Kingdom of this World.* London: A. R. Mowbray and Co., 1958, p. 69.

Moreover, the theory that matter acts dialectically is not substantiated by atomic physics. As Lester DeKoster notes: "A mental contradiction is understandable; the tension and opposition between physical forces is also understandable; but to suppose that these physical contradictions arise by *self*-contradiction, and are resolved when some third force arises which absorbs something real from each of the competing forces is the gratuitous imposition upon physics of concepts which take real and meaningful significance only in mind."[3]

Marx himself was more of an idealist than he was willing to admit. He was nurtured on the German idealism of Hegel and Fichte, and never fully succeeded in freeing himself from their influence. The idealistic strain in Marxism coupled with activism turns out to be a form of existential philosophy which denies absolute objective reality. If man as subject can change the world of objects, then this is a contradiction of the law of necessity which has little lasting significance.

Marx claimed to have discovered the scientific laws of history in his theory of dialectical materialsm. If it were a "scientific" interpretation of history, Marx could have accurately predicted the trend of history. What Marx did was to take arbitrarily the system of Hegel and force it to fit his theory. Thus he only selected a few facts to support his assumptions regarding the movement of the dialectic. Therefore, he could make no scientific prediction as to the course or trend of history. For example, Marx predicted that communism would come to those countries where capitalism was fully matured; it came instead to Russia and China, both of which were pre-capitalistic countries. Marx predicted a progressive polarization of a few rich and the poverty-stricken masses resulting in revolution and the overthrow of the capitalists; there came instead a modification of capitalism through powerful trade unions, legislative control, improved labor-management relations, and the rise of a broad base of the middle class with millions of shareholders in great businesses and industrial corporations.

Marx predicted that in a communist society there would be

[3]*Communism and Christian Faith.* Grand Rapids, Michigan: Wm. B. Eerdmans Publishing Co., 1962, p. 97.

no need for the state; in every country captured by the communists, however, the state has become absolute and totalitarian. Marx predicted that in a communist society there would be freedom, creativity, happiness, and plenty for all; the exact opposite has happened. There is no equality, freedom, plenty, creativity, or wide-spread happiness under communist regimes.

Marx claimed that the dialectic of history would cease in a classless society. Theoretically this may be convincing, but it does not work out in a practical situation. A classless society is impossible and only fanatical communists would deny the fact that in the Soviet Union there is intense class struggle with only a few belonging to the privileged class.

The fact is that no one is able to determine which stage in history is thesis, antithesis, or synthesis. It is an unending stream of which no one knows the beginning or end. As R. N. Carew Hunt points out, history provides no *terminus a quo,* making it impossible to determine which of its stages is thesis, antithesis, and synthesis.[4] Moreover there is no objective standard by which we can assess the progress of history and the stage at which it has arrived at any particular time.

Thus Marx's optimistic theory of continuous historical progress has no foundation in fact. History is not a clear-cut success story. There is no scientific evidence that history moves from thesis, antithesis, to a "higher form" of synthesis. History, in fact, is characterized by decay and decline for which the dialectic has no explanation. While there is evidence of "progress" in the realm of technology, there is no sure evidence of a corresponding progress in morality. Indeed, with every increasing possibility of moral progress there is a corresponding possibility of retrogression. World Wars I, II, and the possibility of a global war and its accompanying horrors, should be sufficient to explode any overly optimistic view that history is moving inevitably toward social utopia.

Actually the Marxist philosophy of history would have little appeal if it were not shot through with a prophetic and messianic element which provides communism with its most powerful dy-

[4]*The Theory and Practice of Communism.* New York: Macmillan Co., 1961, p. 44.

namic. Marx secularized the messianism of the Old Testament, and, as Berdyaev has well said: "It is not the scientific consciousness of Marxism which gives it a revolutionary dynamic, but its messianic expectation."[5] Economic determinism, the class struggle, and the hope of a classless society, would have little appeal apart from this messianic element in Marxism. And it is obvious that the messianic element has nothing to do with science nor can it be verified in the purely empirical method.

2. Marxist Economic Theory

Marxian economic determinism in which is stressed the economic factor in the character and role of history is oversimplified. Economics is a complex reality and to single out one factor as "the cause" to the exclusion of others in the formation of culture and society is to fall into a particularized and fallacious view of the whole process.

The heart of Marxist economics is the theory of surplus value. Marx declared that surplus value is that value which is above what is necessary for the worker's subsistence and is pocketed by the capitalist, but rightly belongs to the worker. But capital is also the product of labor and, without capital, labor could not exist. The surplus value theory overlooks the fact that the capitalist not only works but runs a risk when investing his capital in machinery and land.

Ironically, in the Soviet Union the worker does not get the surplus value which he produces. Surplus goes to a state capitalistic system. Indeed much more goes to the state than goes to the capitalist in the free world. Those who would abolish the free enterprise system must bear in mind that there is no guarantee that under a communist system there will be fewer economic evils. And they should bear in mind also that one thing is certain: namely, that the workers in a totalitarian state are completely regimented and exploited by the Communist Party.

3. The Communist View of the State

As we have seen, the State in the thought of the communist is

[5]The Realm of the Spirit and the Realm of Caesar. New York: Harper and Brothers, 1952, pp. 129-30.

an organ in the hands of the owners to exploit the workers. It developed out of the desire of the possessing class to exploit the non-possessing class. In other words, the State was "invented" by the owners to protect their interest and to rule the workers.[6] It is now generally agreed by political theorists that the factors of kinship and neighborhood led to the formation of communities which became States when customs and taboos were formalized and entrusted to authority for enforcement.[7]

Marxists declare that the state will "wither away." They argue that it cannot but cease to exist because there will be no exploitation in the new communist society.[8] The State will be able to wither away completely when society can apply the rule: "From each according to his ability, to each according to his needs."[9]

But actually what has happened in all countries where communists have taken over is that the State has become all-powerful. Statism is implicit in the Marxist requirements of total planning, monopolistic control, and political power in the hands of communist leaders.[10] Under Lenin the dictatorship of the proletariat became the dictatorship of the party. Exploitation of the worker has not been abolished. Rather, the police state prevails and exploitation of the worker is in evidence on every hand. Lenin himself did not believe that the workers were capable of administering the State. And Khrushchev has made it clear that it would be a gross mistake to weaken the State in the Soviet Union today. Moreover there is only the promise of the Kremlin leaders that the State will gradually wither away as the danger of attack from outside diminishes.

[6]Friedrich Engels, *Origin of the Family, Private Property and The State,* trans. by Ernest Untermann. Chicago: Charles Kerr and Co., 1902, pp. 131ff.

[7]Wallace S. Sayer, *American Government.* New York: Barnes and Noble Incorporated, 1961, p. 5.

[8]V. I. Lenin, "State and Revolution," *Selected Works,* n.d., Vol. VII, p. 24.

[9]*Ibid.,* p. 87ff.

[10]Henry Mayo, *Introduction to Marxist Theory.* New York: Oxford University Press, 1960, p. 270.

4. Marxist View of Man

Communist anthropology betrays certain basic weaknesses. Marx claims that man is primarily a product of history. He is the sum total of social-economic relations. His self-realization comes through his work and ownership of the means of production.[11] So it is the economic basis that largely determines the shape of man. Therefore, Marx's doctrine is not so much anthropocentric as sociocentric. Marx's man, as Berdyaev declares, "has lost the image and likeness of God; he is the image and likeness of society. He is entirely a product of his social surroundings, of the economics of his epoch and class to which he belongs."[12] Thus the individual is lost in society and has no significance apart from it.

Marx's naivete about human nature is pointed up in the optimistic view that, once the capitalist society is banished and the communist society is established, man will transcend his self-interest and be "naturally" good. Such a view overlooks the fact that man will carry his greed and selfishness into the communist utopia. Robinson has put the whole matter in graphic terms:

> The materials upon which the Communist has to draw for reconstruction of the world must still be quarried from the same pit of unregenerate human nature. The contractors are still the same old Adam and Sons, whose houses since the beginning have been founded on the sands of self-interest, corruption, and waste, and have persistently cracked and tumbled to decay.[13]

Thus the Achilles' heel of communism is in its naive view of man. It has no understanding of the radical nature of sin. It assumes that man is inherently good and, once transplanted into the good environment, will automatically blossom into a good person. History refutes this extremely optimistic view of human

[11]Karl Marx, "Economic and Philosophical Manuscripts," trans. by T. B. Bottomore, in Erich Fromm, *Marx's Concept of Man*. New York: Frederick Ungar Publishing Company, 1961, pp. 93-196.

[12]*The Russian Revolution*, pp. 78-79.

[13]John A. T. Robinson, "The Christian Hope" in D. M. MacKinnon, *Christian Faith and Communist Faith*. London: Macmillan and Company, 1953, p. 218.

nature. There seems to be little evidence that man has been improved in his basic nature even in the socialist society of the Soviet Union.

5. Communist Strategies and Tactics

Communism's inhumane methods of expansion cannot be justified on the ground of reason or religion. To gain their ends, communists use terror, force, the big lie, murder, slave labor, secret police, and any other means at their command. Such methods can be freely used since morality for the communists is whatever promotes their cause. At the same time the communists make moral pretensions of brotherhood, equality, and justice, holding out the promise of a social utopia on earth.

Some intellectuals with a passion for justice, brotherhood, freedom, and the end of poverty, at one time thought that communism was the way to achieve these goals. But they discovered that these terms were merely "catchwords" and that "truth" is whatever the Party says it is at any moment. Andre Gide, the French author, was one of these. Converted to communism, he went to Russia in June, 1936, full of high hopes. He returned a disappointed and disillusioned man declaring: "There was in my Soviet adventure something tragic. I had arrived there a convinced and enthusiastic follower in order to admire a new world, and they offered me, to tempt me and win me, all the prerogatives and privileges which I had abhorred in the old world."[14] Everywhere Gide saw the same gulf which separates the privileged from the underprivileged, along with inequalities, lack of freedom of thought and opinion, and widespread oppression.

Likewise, countries drawn into the communist orbit experience disillusionment. Farmers of such nations who are promised land find themselves without land and subject to collectivization and coercion. Nationalists who succumb to communist appeals to liberation discover that they are colonialized by new and harsher masters. The communist "classless" society turns out to be a new privileged class, the Party bosses. The glorified "workers

[14]Richard Crossman, ed., *The God That Failed,* p. 174.

state" degenerates into a situation where the worse exploitation of early capitalism is combined with terrors of the police state. Ironically Marx's criticism of capitalism as exploitation—"The proletariat gets for his labor only the minimum necessary for his existence . . . all surplus is taken by the employer"—obtains in every communist country today. Now it is the communist state which takes the surplus value and leaves the worker with barely enough to live on. In captured communist countries, people find themselves not individual persons of concern to the Party, but things to be used by the Party. In short, these gullible countries find that the "cure" is more evil than the disease.

Charges of colonialism, imperialism, racism, and economic injustice by the communists against Western nations is hypocritical. It is true that the way in which Western nations sliced off spheres of influence and exploited weaker countries such as Africa and Asia makes a sorry chapter in history of the West. Communists never mention the values which were brought to these subjugated countries by the West. Nor do the communists mention the fact that most Western powers have abandoned their policies of colonialization, granting freedom to many countries when they were ready for self-government.

The hypocrisy of the communists in making such charges is seen in the fact that they themselves are now the imperialists and colonialists. For example, the Soviets have their satellites in Eastern Europe and China has hers in North Korea, North Vietnam, and Tibet. It must be noted also that minority groups in every communist country suffer persecution and discrimination. For example, the Jews in the Soviet Union are the most persecuted people in that country. And all religious groups suffer from the limitations imposed upon them by the State.

Communism has a naive view of sin and evil. Marx's tendency to think of the proletariat as sinless and the owner as the sinner is erroneous. Sin for Marx was exploitation by the capitalists of the sinless proletariat. He held that once the individual is in the communist society he will be transformed into a real man. He will achieve human status, leaving behind him selfishness and greed. But the self which he takes into utopia is still the same sinful self.

Marx was able to hold to his theory of the goodness of the proletariat because he located evil in the form of economic relations in society. His naivete with reference to sin is seen in the fact that he believed that evil could be eliminated simply by changing the form of economic relations. Hence the proletariat escapes from any responsibility for evil. The worker is simply a victim of estrangement because he has been alienated from the sources of production. Salvation will come when the means of production are restored to him.

And finally, communism is atheistic. As a consequence it has no real answer to many of the basic questions of human existence. It has no answer to the problem of creation. The writer recalls the pathetic attempt of a young communist in Moscow to explain the origin of things. She declared that there are "creative forces in matter." But when asked where the creative forces came from, there appeared a blank expression on her face. Communists claim that God is simply a mythical, invented being. God is man made in his own image, a fantastic mirror image of a human being. Therefore, belief in God is incompatible with materialism. And since the communists reject belief in God, they have deified matter. Dialectical materialism, a finite theory, is made absolute. This is nothing less than idolatry.

Since communists reject the idea of God, they have no answer to tragedy, especially the tragedy of death. A student in the Warsaw University asked his professor to explain the meaning of life and death. At first the professor thought the student was baiting him, but looking around he saw many eyes watching attentively and he knew that this was a serious question from all of the students. The professor concluded that the Marxist philosophy should "as quickly as possible and on a wide a scale as possible take up the problem of the human individual and his fate, previously neglected by it, though evoking such a broad response."[15]

Marx described religion as the "opium of the people" to keep them drugged and to prevent them from demanding justice of their exploiters. But this is precisely what communism is and does. It is the opium of the conscience, making it possible for

[15]*Time*, June 2, 1961, pp. 58-63.

communists to commit all kinds of evil in the name of communist causes. It is a chloroform which stultifies the minds and the spirits of the people, keeping them from rising up against a tyrannical, oppressive government which promises the good life in the near future.

Communism turns out to be a demonic religion, promising a perfect society which is continually postponed with each generation. But communists cannot go on perpetually delaying the coming of social utopia. Eventually the masses may see communism for what it really is: "the wolf of Nazism disguised as the sheep of perfection."[16]

[16]T. V. Smith and Eduard Lindeman, *The Democratic Way of Life*. New York: Mentor Book, New American Library of World Literature, Inc., 1951, p. 98.

CHAPTER VI

Communism and the Clergy

Certain leading theologians have responded to communism in various ways. Some have given an absolute "No" to the movement. Others have sought a *modus vivendi*, a mode of life, acceptable to both the Christian religion and the Communist regime. Representative among these theologians are Emil Brunner, Hewlett Johnson, Joseph Hromadka, Reinhold Niebuhr, and Karl Barth.

1. Emil Brunner: An Absolute No

Among those clergymen who think of communism as a total enemy of the church and the free world is Emil Brunner, Swiss theologian and formerly professor at the University of Zurich. He is alarmed at the success communism has gained in the world of Protestantism. The World Council of Churches, he complains, has accepted as a password: "Anti-Communism is the line of the Roman Catholic Church and must inevitably lead to war." As a result, Brunner claims that the idea has become widespread that anti-communism is unworthy of a Christian, and that one has to "remain in communication with communism." Furthermore, acceptance of churches into the World Council from Iron Curtain countries disturbs Brunner. He claims that their delegates are subservient to the communist state. And Brunner has been severely critical of Karl Barth, a leading spokesman for Protestantism, for being neutral and "soft" on communism.[1]

Brunner conceives communism to be totalitarian through and through and, as such, is an unjust, inhuman, and godless state. Communism possesses so completely everyone and everything that it is the worst form of tyranny. It controls everything for the purpose of producing a new type of humanity. The new man

[1]"An Open Letter to Karl Barth," in Karl Barth, *Against the Stream, Shorter Post-War Writings, 1946-1952.* New York: Philosophical Library, 1954, pp. 106-113.

it seeks to create is devoid of all that is human. Therefore, communism is a denial of individual freedom and dignity. It is atheistic and seeks to destroy all religions. Moreover, it is more evil than Nazism, which Barth challenged and was forced to leave Germany for doing so.

For these and other reasons Brunner holds that the church cannot remain "neutral," but must join in the struggle of the free world to maintain its basic traditions of freedom, human dignity, human rights, and democracy.

The theological response of Brunner to communism finds its ground in obedience to the divine command of God in Christ. Brunner reduces all the commands of God to love of God and neighbor. To love God and neighbor is the will of God and the norm of the Good. The Good is simply what God *wills* that we should do in terms of love. And since we know God's will only through his revelation, his command is primarily a gift and, as such, a demand. To know God in his action by faith, and to participate in this action, is the supreme Good. Thus, Brunner defines Christian ethics as "the science of human conduct as it is determined by Divine conduct."[2] The Good, then consists not in a principle, but in always doing what God wills at any particular moment under the guidance of the Spirit.

To avoid the ambiguities related to natural law, Brunner places emphasis upon the orders of creation, that is, the family, the state, the economic order, culture, and the church. He believes that it is the will of God to preserve orders which make for community. The new man in Christ is to serve within these orders, transforming them by love to neighbor.

The unalterable basic forms of these orders are the gifts of the Creator and preserve the world; but the forms in which they appear at any given time, which is constantly changing their historically concrete form, is due to the effect of human sin, and is therefore, like all that is sinful, the object of moral conflict. Even the permanent forms of these orders, as in the case of all that is historical, express the inherited curse of sin. Everyone who participates in them participates in sin. To run away from

[2]*The Divine Imperative.* Trans. by Olive Wyon. Philadelphia: Westminister Press, 1947, p. 86.

them is to fall into a more radical sin of the loss of community. Thus, one must live in the world without being of it.[3]

Love is the criterion of conduct within these orders. But love needs justice and, without it, becomes mere sentimentality. Justice means to render to every man his due. But love can never do less than justice. Love only begins where justice has already been done, "for it is that which is beyond justice."[4]

These orders are not merely human creations and human tasks, but divine creations and divine gifts. And since they are gifts of God they are also sacred tasks. Thus the Christian must work within these orders transforming them by the expression of love to God and neighbor.

Brunner recognizes that no Christian program exists, and yet we are to constantly seek a better social order. In his judgment it is impossible to lay down once and for all the "laws" of a Christian society, but in each fresh historical situation work for a better society.

Brunner proceeds, therefore, cautiously to suggest some general criteria for a Christian civilization. There is the principle of federalism, a pluralism of communities—family, customs, rites —prior to the state to be co-ordinated by the state but never to be dominated by it. Again, there is the principle of personal freedom in community which requires the limitation of those powers, economic and political, which deprive persons of free participation and responsibility in community. And, finally, there is the principle of justice which does not mean equality. While all have equality before God, the rights of the Christian depend upon his place in the family, his service at work and in the community.

Thus Brunner's answer to communist ideology and strategy is largely individualistic and conservative. For him, the Christian is to serve within the orders, improving the situation by personally infusing the Spirit of Christ into the social order. He thinks that the church does her most effective social transformation by equipping her members with the Spirit of Christ and uniting the

[3]*Ibid.*, p. 338.
[4]*Justice and the Social Order.* New York: Harper and Brothers, 1945, p. 130.

capitalists and workers in the common search for a better society. Nobody knows what this order will be like, but it certainly will be "neither totalitarianism nor *laissez faire* liberalism."[5]

Brunner is to be commended for solidly grounding the Christian response to communism in theology. However, there are definite practical limitations in his approach to communism. While he is absolutely opposed to communism, he lacks a positive strategy in meeting its challenge.

Brunner's conservatism expresses itself in his emphasis on the individualistic approach of transforming society, overlooking the vexing problem of power. He allows for only a "limited reform" within the orders of creation through individual effort. Moreover, he is vague as to how this reform is to be achieved. Likewise, his principles of what a Christian civilization is to be like are unclear and he fails to provide a positive means for the achievement of such a civilization.

Brunner's absolute "No" to communism tends to ignore the fact that communists themselves are human beings for whom Christ died. His approach prevents one from understanding the problems of individuals in communist countries and taking positive steps to give them aid and hope.

And finally, Brunner fails to appreciate the achievements under communist regimes in terms of education, science, and industry. While these are acquired at the expense of freedom and great suffering on the part of the people, one cannot ignore the fact that great strides have been made in these areas.

2. Hewlett Johnson: Yes to Communism

Some religious thinkers attempt to reconcile Christianity and communism on the basis of liberal theology. Representative of these men is Hewlett Johnson, popularly known as the "Red Dean." His leftist affiliations and actions as Dean of Canterbury of the Anglican communion in England has earned him this title.

Johnson came from a cotton manufacturing family in Manchester and worked as an engineer before studying theology at

[5]*Communism, Capitalism, and Christianity.* London: Lutterworth Press, 1949, pp. 43-44.

Oxford. For many years he has served on the editorial board of *The Daily Worker,* the British Communist Party newspaper. He has attended peace rallies from Peking to New York where he was royally entertained by the Reds. In 1950 he was awarded the Stalin Peace Prize. In 1952 Johnson visited the communist side in the Korean War and accused the Americans of germ warfare, a charge later abandoned by the communists.

In 1948 Johnson was denied a visa to the United States by the State Department. He was to be the guest of the National Council of Churches of Christ. Finally, a visa was granted to him to come on a personal visit. In 1959 his book, *The Upsurge of China,* was banned from India because two of its maps showed Indian territory as a part of Red China. Thus Johnson's political views have been a constant source of embarrassment to the Church of England, but his ecclesiastical superiors endured his outspoken championship of communism. All were happy when he resigned as Dean of Canterbury in 1963 at the age of 88.

Johnson practically equates Christian ethics with communism, claiming that the latter is following the standard of Christ. He thinks that the communist who feels himself creating a universal brotherhood of mankind or the classless society "has recovered much of the core of real belief in God."[6] In keeping with Christianity, the communist has cut the taproot of covetousness, overcome the fragmentation of life caused by the influence of Greek dualism on Christianity, and in his emphasis on community proves himself to be "heir of the Christian intention," and thereby, "demands Christian recognition."[7] Johnson naively concludes that had Christians recognized the communist motto, "From everyone according to his ability and to everyone according to his needs," is so wholly Christian, and had acted accordingly, the Soviet communists might never have launched a war against religion.[8]

Is Johnson a communist or a misguided liberal Christian? Nikita Khrushchev says that Johnson is not a communist. At

[6]*The Soviet Power.* New York: International Publishers, 1950, p. 315.
[7]*Ibid.,* pp. 318-319.
[8]*Ibid.*

a conference in the Kremlin in 1957, Khrushchev declared: "You probably know the name of Hewlett Johnson. When we were in England and his name came up, he was called the 'Red Dean.' Why? Only because he is a consistent advocate of peace. He is not a communist. It makes us all the more proud when an honest man who is against war is called 'Red.' We greet them though they are not Reds. Johnson is far from it. We differ philosophically, but we agree on one thing—peace."[9]

Khrushchev is no doubt correct in saying that Johnson does not accept the materialistic ideology of communism. It is obvious, however, that he accepts the political action of the communists as the social expression of Christianity. For in his speeches, writings, and actions, Johnson enthusiastically comes to the defense of communist efforts to establish a communist society which he believes is in keeping with Christian faith and principles.

Johnson completely misunderstands the meaning of communism when he attempts to harmonize it with Christian ethics. Since he has never lived under a communist regime, Johnson cannot understand the demonic nature of dimensions of communism. He seems to wholly disregard the fact that communism is anti-Christian and has as its avowed aim to destroy all religions. Also he conveniently avoids denouncing communist methods of terror, oppression, and slavery, which communists impose upon millions of helpless people.

Because of his thin theological orientation, Johnson can identify Christianity with even atheistic communism. He thus falls into the fatal trap of liberal theologians who tend to identify the Kingdom of God with social institutions and progress. In his emphasis upon peace, Johnson fails to see that true peace cannot be had without justice. And to equate Christianity with either capitalism or communism is a distortion which can only be accomplished in the mind and never in the Scriptures.

[9]H. H. Barnette, "Relations with the Russians," *Review and Expositor*, July, 1959, p. 252.

3. Joseph Hromadka: Accept as God's Judgment and Society's Hope

In contrast to those who attempt to reconcile communism and Christianity on the basis of a liberal theology, there are others who respond to communism in terms of a theology of crisis. They see in communism a judgment of God and the divinely-ordained "wave of the future." Joseph Hromadka, Dean of the Comenius Protestant Theological Faculty of Prague, Czechoslovakia, is the chief defender of this position. Though he does not attempt to accommodate Christian theology to communism, he does support the latter as the harbinger of a new age which the church must accept.

Hromadka's thought runs as follows. Civilization is in total crisis. The old world is dying. Western democracies are decadent and lack moral, spiritual, and political strength to cope with the crisis. "We are living," he declares, "on the ruins of the old world, both morally and politically."[10] The spiritual demise of the West is further seen in the rearming of Germany, the refusal to seat Red China in the U.N., lack of support of the Stockholm Peace Appeal, and engagement in the Korean War. Any attempt, believes Hromadka, to save Western civilization by reactionary devices will be futile. But while the situation is dark, it is also promising. Behind the events of current history, "the Risen Lord is doing His work."[11]

In Hromadka's judgment, communism reflects, in a very secularized form, the Christian longing for the fellowship of full and responsible life.[12] However, he does not give complete sanction to communism. At the philosophical level the Christian must say "no" to the claims of the State, the tendency of communism to put class above the individual, and its materialistic ideology.

At the level of practice, Hromadka admits that there are dangers in communism such as the concentration of power in

[10]*Doom and Resurrection.* Richmond: Madrus House, 1945, p. 119.

[11]*Ibid.,* p. 121.

[12]"Between Yesterday and Today," *Christianity and Crisis,* Vol. 8, No. 9, May 24, 1948, p. 67ff.

the hands of the Party and the cruel treatment of minorities.
But he merely bids the Christian to look beyond these factors
to the remarkable economic, scientific, and educational progress
being made by the communists.

The church, Hromadka declares, should warn communists
to avoid injustice and to consider themselves in the service
of men. Appeal should be made to the Soviet leaders to rely
less upon violent methods of agitation, threat, deportation, trials,
police control, and to arouse in man the noblest sentiments of
sympathy for the poor, the weak, the helpless, the miserable,
and to awaken in him the true core of socialistic humanism.[13]
He concludes: "This is a time for hope and for new beginnings.
. . . We cannot make any predictions, but our courage and
hope may pave a new highway for reconciliation and peace."[14]

Hromadka's analysis of communism betrays certain serious
weaknesses. While there is some validity in his comments about
the crisis of the West and the failure of the church to challenge
the evils which characterize it, neither Hromadka nor the church
of Czechoslovakia have protested against the tyrannies of their
communist government. There is apparently no effort of the
church in that country to challenge the evils of communism
and to transform society in terms of Christian principles.

As is well-known today the Stockholm Peace Appeal, and all
other similar efforts participated in by Hromadka, was mere
communist propaganda for Soviet imperialistic efforts to extend
its power over the world.

Moreover, when Hromadka declares that communism is the
secularized form of Christianity and that in time its atheism,
which is allegedly peripheral to the center of communism, will
be sloughed off, he is engaging in wishful thinking. Atheism is
basic to communism which aims to destroy all religious faith.

Hromadka condemns capitalism in the West as being unjust.
On the other hand, he praises communism as being more just.
He does not see that state capitalism is the prevailing eco-
nomic system in the Soviet Union and in his own country.

[13]"Our Responsibility in the Post-War World," *Man's Disorder and
God's Design*. New York: Harper and Brothers, 1948, Vol. 4, pp. 141-142.
[14]*Ibid.*, p. 142.

The Party is the capitalist which employs, controls and operates without competition the entire economy. The Party has simply displaced the old capitalists and rules the workers with an iron fist. Workers have no right to strike against the government or industries. And finally, there is a dualism in Hromadka's Christian faith. Theology is in one compartment and has little or no relationship to government, economics, and social life.

4. Reinhold Niebuhr: Yes, then No

Among those theologians who have become enamored with Marxism as a means of ushering in a more just society is Reinhold Niebuhr, Professor Emeritus of Union Theological Seminary in New York City. To understand his response to communism, it is necessary to consider his concern for bridging the gap between Christian love and social realities.

Niebuhr's social concern grew out of his experience as pastor for thirteen years of a Lutheran church in Detroit, Michigan. This church was almost in the shadow of the great Ford factories. The social realities of the rapidly expanding industrial community with its concomitant problems of unemployment, inadequate wages, loss of homes, along with the disillusions growing out of World War I, forced Niebuhr to rethink his liberal theology upon which he had been bred.

In the process of rethinking his theology, Niebuhr moved toward a deeper stage of political realism and Biblical theology. In the early 1930's he discovered a useful tool in Marxism. He was convinced that any radical reconstruction of the social order from capitalism to socialism could not be effected by democracy alone.[15] Hence, in revolutionary Marxism he thought that he had found a more adequate guide to economic and political reform. In his own words, Niebuhr explains that he "used Marxist collectivism to counter liberal individualism, Marxist catastrophism to counter liberal optimism, and Marxist determinism to challenge liberal moralism and idealism."[16] In

[15]*Reflections on the End of an Era.* New York: Charles Scribner's Sons, 1934, pp. 156-157.

[16]"Communism and the Clergy," *Christian Century*, Vol. LXX, No. 33, August 19, 1953, p. 937.

the new society, Niebuhr believed, the workers would be the rulers. For him the old bourgeois society was finished. The logic of history, he felt, affirmed this type of new order.

But Niebuhr never fully accepted Marxism. He saw the error of the communists who found the "Kingdom of God" *in* history. And though for a while he regarded this communist error as an indispensable myth, an illusion of the moment for the realization of justice, he had reservations about other aspects of communism.[17] By 1935 he had repudiated the myth by declaring: "I once thought such a faith could be harmless illusion. But now I see that its net result is to endow a group of oligarchs with the religious sanctity which primitive priest-kings once held."[18]

Also Niebuhr saw that communism jeopardized human freedom and tended toward a new pattern of privilege and power. In this Niebuhr was prophetic, for today the Party is made up of the privileged and those who wield absolute power in all communist countries. The climax of Niebuhr's critique of communism appeared in 1953 when he branded it as a secular religion characterized by a "noxious demonry." In answer to the question as to why communism is so evil, he cited four aspects of it: (1) its monopoly of power, growing out of the doctrine of the "dictatorship of the proletariat; (2) its utopian illusions which provide a moral facade for the most unscrupulous political policies; (3) its belief in the transformation of society by revolution, after which man is no longer the creature but the creator of history both proposing and disposing; and (4) the pretension of scientific rationality.[19]

Thus Niebuhr took the Marxist views of the logic of history, the doctrine of class conflict, and the emphasis on the role of force. Later he rejected the Marxist logic of history, reduced the idea of class conflict to a subordinate place, but held on to the concept of power and force minus its Marxist meaning.

[17]*Moral Man and Immoral Society.* New York: Charles Scribner's Sons, 1949, p. 277.

[18]"Religion and Marxism," *Modern Monthly,* February, 1935.

[19]*Christian Realism and Political Problems.* New York: Charles Scribner's Sons, 1953, pp. 34-42.

He still holds that all justice in human society rests upon some kind of balance of power.

In 1940 Niebuhr resigned from the Socialist Party and gave support to F. D. Roosevelt's New Deal. At first he had vigorously opposed the New Deal as a kind of "whirligig reform."[20] Now he became a New Dealer, giving ardent support to the new political movement.[21]

But in 1947, Niebuhr still considered himself a socialist in the sense that property must be socialized where it makes for injustice through inordinate centralization.[22] At this time he became a leading figure in Americans for Democratic Action, an organization dedicated to pragmatic, piecemeal, and gradual reform. Thus, he gave up socialism as an expression of historical judgment and hope in our time. And eventually he came to feel that the New Deal of Roosevelt might be a viable middle way between capitalism and socialism.

Niebuhr's subsequent writings have developed this "middle way" position. He now feels that we have attained a measure of equilibrium in economic society by setting organized power over against organized power. Where this has not been sufficient, political power has been used to redress disproportions and disbalances in economic society.[23]

Such is the response of an American theologian to communism. One of his basic weaknesses is that he tends to take his ethical, social imperatives from history instead of from the individual's relation to Christ. Once he saw in Marxism an instrument of Christian ethics; now he attempts to find God's will in a pragmatic, democratic tradition. His ethics, therefore, is derived largely from the historical, concrete situation, though he does hold that all individuals and institutions stand under the criticism of transcendent love.

Again, we have noted that Niebuhr rejected the Marxist myth of utopia in society, but he has failed in his theology to

[20]"Roosevelt's Merry-Go-Round," *Radical Religion*, Spring, 1938.

[21]"An End to Illusion," *Nation*, June, 1940.

[22]Editorial, "Frontier Fellowship," *Christianity and Society*, Vol. 13, No. 4, Autumn, 1948, p. 3.

[23]*Christian Realism and Political Problems. Op. cit.*, p. 50.

provide a hope in history of a better society which would moti-
vate needed radical social change. All hope of a redeemed
society is projected against a suprahistory. Hence, he does not
provide an answer to the communist promise of a new and
just society here and now which affords such a powerful in-
centive for social action.

Rather, Niebuhr puts his hope in the genius of the democratic
society to develop organic institutions capable of balancing
power with power, economic, political, religious, and social;
and, as Charles West observes, Niebuhr provides little help
for Christians in communist countries. He does not emphasize
the Christian's personal witness to communists, but lays stress
on the political factor. Also he has little to say about the
response of the church under communism. What is to be the
ministry of the church where it is dominated by tyrannical
power and where Christians suffer and have no political power?[24]

5. Karl Barth: Wait and See or "Neutralism"

Without question Karl Barth is the foremost Protestant theologian today. Born in Basel, Switzerland in 1886, he served as
pastor of a church from 1911 to 1921. Subsequently, he became
a Professor of Theology in the German University of Bonn.
Because of his stand against Nazism and his refusal to take
the oath of allegiance to Adolf Hitler, Barth was dismissed
from his professorship and went to the University of Basel
where he now holds a professorship in theology.

Barth's position on communism is most clearly presented in
his works *Against the Stream* and in *How to Serve God In A
Marxist Land*. Emil Brunner[25] has raised the question why Barth
has not summoned the church to an absolute "no!" to communism as he did in the case of Hitlerism. He makes several
observations to establish the question. He declares that Barth:
(1) hardly ever attacks the inhumanity inherent in the nature
of totalitarianism; (2) that he displaces the problem of a totali-

[24]*Communism and the Theologians.* Philadelphia: Westminister Press,
pp. 174-176.

[25]"An Open Letter to Karl Barth," in Karl Barth, *Against the Stream:
Shorter Post-War Writings,* 1946-52, pp. 106-113.

tarian state by the problem of "East and West" and the problem
of communism, when it is also a problem of the church; (3)
that he talks about communism which the church should not
reject outright, even though it is totalitarian; (4) that he justifies
the rejection of a full "no" to communism by referring to the
social injustice in the West; (5) that he is a socialist and
socialism is in a death struggle with communism; (6) that he
fails to denounce communism despite the fact that it is atheistic
and denies basic human rights, even as Nazism; (7) that he
asserts that communism realizes certain social postulates which
the church must welcome, an argument which was heard in
the Hitler state; (8) that he defends communism as a "historical
necessity" because democracy has failed, a position of which a
Protestant theologian should be ashamed; (9) that he advocates
that Protestants should not attack communism because the
Catholic Church does; and (10) that collaboration of Christian
leaders in Hungary to which Barth gave at least tacit approval
has resulted in many people turning away from the church
because they feel they are betraying the cause of freedom.

Prodded by Brunner's question as to why he is uncritical of
communism, Barth gives his answer in a personal letter and
elaborates on the problem in other writings. He is not "rousing"
the church to oppose communism for several reasons. In his
judgment, the present struggle between Russia and the United
States is a struggle between children who have suddenly become
giants and want to master each other, with Europe in an unfortunate position between them.[26] The Christian attitude
in this conflict is to refrain from fright and to avoid taking
part in it. Both East and West, America and Russia, are hurling
accusations against each other and pointing out each other's
weaknesses. The first element of our Christian political attitude
is refusal to fight one way or the other in this conflict. For the
church is *not* identical with the West, and the Western conscience and judgment is not necessarily the Christian judgment.
Nor is the Christian judgment and the Christian conscience
necessarily the Eastern conscience and judgment either. Thus

[26]*Ibid.*, p. 129.

the church is to remain aloof in the quarrel between the two great world powers today. It is Barth's opinion that the church today "ought to stand quietly aloof from the present conflict and not let off all its guns before it is necessary but wait calmly to see whether and in what sense the situation will grow serious again and call for speech."[27]

Another reason why Barth is not attacking communism as he did Nazism is that the latter tried to represent and recommend itself in the guise of a falsified Christianity while communism makes no pretension of being Christian. During the Nazi regime in Germany, Hitler had become a spiritual and political source of temptation. People were in danger of complete sacrifice to national socialism. Communism has never attempted to shroud itself in a Christian garment. It has never committed the basic crime of the Nazis by removing and replacing the real Christ by a national Jesus, and it has never committed the crime of anti-Semitism. There is nothing of the false prophet about it. Communism is not anti-Christian; it is coldly non-Christian and honestly Godless.[28] Thus the Christian is not tempted by communism nor is the church threatened as in the case of Nazism.

Moreover, Barth thinks that there is a "positive intention" behind Soviet "totalitarian atrocities." Thus one cannot say of communism what one was forced to say of Nazism—that what it means and intends is pure unreason, the product of madness and crime. It would be absurd to speak in the same breath about the philosophy of Marxism and the ideology of the Third Reich, to mention a man of stature such as Joseph Stalin in the same breath as such charlatans as Hitler and his cohorts. And while what has been tackled in Soviet Russia with very dirty and bloody hands, and in a way that rightly shocks us—is, after all, a constructive idea, "the solution of a problem which is a serious and burning problem for us as well, and which we with our clean hands have not yet tackled anything like energetically enough: the social problem."[29]

[27]*Ibid.*, p. 117.
[28]*Ibid.*, p. 140.
[29]*Ibid.*, p. 139.

All of this does not mean that the church is uninterested in political events. But today it is not a question of struggle, but of reconstruction for which Christians must be responsible in the political world. The Christian church stands for reconstruction and therefore cannot agree with one side and disagree with the other. Both East and West seem to be concerned with humanity and faith. For both sides accuse each other of inhumanity and false belief. Thus, Barth concludes: "The Christian church can therefore stand neither against the West nor the East. It can only walk between the two and call men back to humanity, and that is its contribution to reconstruction.[30]

In 1948, Johannes Hamel, a pastor in East Germany, writing on behalf of other pastors, requested that Barth provide some counsel about how to proclaim the gospel in an Iron Curtain country. Ten years later Barth replied in a "Letter To A Pastor In The German Democratic Republic." After greeting the pastor, Barth sets forth a theological basis for living in a troubled world. Citing I Peter 5:8-9, he points out that the "roaring lion" is at work in the West as well as in the East. Hence, the Western lion must be resisted as well as the Eastern lion. And while aware that the Christians in East Germany are undergoing a painful process of purification and fiery refining, he predicts that the Western world also will not escape sooner or later in some form this same sort of purification, perhaps at the hands of Asia and Africa![31] Barth urges the pastor to read Jeremiah 29 for the proper attitude of the Christian to an alien power. This chapter describes the exiled Hebrews in Babylon. Then he reminds the pastor that God is sovereign even over atheism and materialism. Besides, God is for the atheist as well as the Christian. The church must never "resist" by returning measure for measure. It must "resist" only by being "firm in the faith," never in the name of any principles or dogmas, in an attempt to compel anyone to recognize them in theory and practice.[32]

Barth is in general agreement with the idea that we have

[30]*Ibid.*, pp. 144-145.
[31]*How to Serve God in a Marxist Land*. New York: Association Press, 1959, p. 55.
[32]*Ibid.*, p. 60.

come to the "end of the Constantinian era" in which the church
will no longer be coddled by the state. Indeed, God may have
already begun to put an end to our mode of existence because
it lacks integrity and has lost its usefulness. One day it may
entirely disappear and we definitely should look about us for
new ventures in new directions. And he reminds the Christians
in East Germany that their special calling may be to be a
living example for the rest of the Christians of how a church
lives that seeks for, and perhaps has already entered upon a
new way.[33]

Barth then turns to eight specific questions posed by the East
German pastor. He declares that: Obedience to the gospel must
take precedence over the desire for Germany's reunification
after the pattern of Western prosperity and freedom; there
should be no difficulty in the East German pastors signing the
required loyalty oath of the East German communist government, even though he does not know its specific content; that
it would not be wise to "pray away" the communist government
for the Lord might hear and they could wake up some morning
in the midst of the "flesh-pots of Egypt" and committed to
the "American way of life"; curtailment of the church's right
to freedom and to speak out in public is no ground for resist-
ance even in the face of anti-communist propaganda; they
return to the Word of God, submit to "endurance tests" which
grate on their nerves, and lead to almost irreconcilable differences rather than making their own better knowledge prevail;
the church is not permitted to practice self-defense, but to set
its eyes "straight toward Jerusalem"; the hour for extensive
reconstruction of the church has not struck in East Germany,
and, therefore, the necessity and freedom for immediate and
concrete decisions, which are not possible without prayer, should
be made; and that pastors who have fled from East Germany
leaving their congregations have disposed themselves from office.
In conclusion, Barth reminds the East German pastors that those
in West Germany have their trials and problems also in coping
with the "roaring lion" referred to in I Peter 5:8-9. For they
are in hand to hand combat "with the powers and principalities,

[33]*Ibid.*, pp. 64-65.

the spirits and demons in the land of 'economic miracle' with its thoughtless participation in NATO, with its remilitarization, its military chaplaincy contract, its preparation for atomic armament, its panicky fear of Russia, its crusading moods, its old Nazis. . . ."[34]

Such is the response of Karl Barth to communism. It is puzzling to most of his readers that he does not see the same dangers in communist totalitarianism that he saw in Nazi totalitarianism. It is true that he has made some repudiations of the communist "way of life" as not conforming to "our standards of justice and freedom."[35] Yet, while the same evils of Nazism are characteristic of Soviet communism, Barth generally keeps silent about them. He aroused the church against Nazism but refuses to arouse the church against communism, advising the church to tend to her own affairs and keep silent. This, in spite of the fact that he once saw the "democratic conception of the State" as a "justifiable expansion of the thought of the New Testament" and defended the democratic state against "Facism and Bolshevism alike."[36] And in 1946 Barth declared that the church will certainly "withdraw from and oppose any out-and-out dictatorship such as the totalitarian state."[37] He even chided those who were unable to make a political distinction between facism and communism as men living in a "night in which all cats are gray."[38] With reference to totalitarian communism he now urges "neutralism."

It is strange that Barth had no statement to make about the Hungarian Revolt. When the Hungarian workers made an attempt to oust the Soviet communists, Barth had not a word to say in protest against the Soviet slaughter which followed.[39]

[34]*Ibid.*, p. 78.

[35]*Against the Stream*, *op. cit.*, p. 116.

[36]*Church and State*. London: SCM Press, 1939, pp. 80, 84.

[37]"Christian Community and Civil Government," *Community, State, and Church*. New York: Doubleday and Co., 1960, p. 174.

[38]*Ibid.*, p. 119.

[39]"Barth on Hungary: An Exchange," *The Christian Century*, April 10, 1957, pp. 453-454; see also Reinhold Niebuhr, "Why Barth's Silence on Hungary?" *Ibid.*, January 23, 1957.

Again, it is strange that his christological theology affords no theological sanction for a condemnation of communism. He says, "I cannot admit that it is the duty of Christians or of the Church to give theological backing to what every citizen can, with much shaking of the head, read in his daily paper and what is so admirably expressed by Mr. Truman and by the Pope."[40]

Bartn claims that communism is not "anti-Christian," in spite of the fact that the communists have attempted for years to completely exterminate Christianity and the church in the Soviet Union as well as in other communist countries.

Barth's statement that the Soviet communists have never committed the crime of anti-Semitism is pathetic. He made the statement at the very moment Stalin was engaged in a campaign to completely exterminate the Jews as "rootless cosmopolitans" and "homeless intellectuals." And today the Jews are the most persecuted people in the Soviet Union. There is an all-out campaign to eliminate root and branch the Jewish faith in that country.

Again, Barth's self-righteous attitude and caustic remarks about America and the American way of life are not completely justified. After his visit to America in 1962, he wrote an article entitled "Remembrances of America," in which he admitted that he knew "too little about America to be able to speak completely about it."[41] But his anti-American statements would lead the reader to think that he was thoroughly familar with "the American way of life."

Again, Barth's letter to the pastors in the German republic, as he admits, is based on a lack of detailed information. And yet he gives some astonishingly specific answers to the questions posed. But many of his answers were vague and general. In his reply to Karl Barth from East Germany, Johannes Hamel declared: "Once again you seem to have chosen to sit on the fence, and, like a lonely bird on a rooftop, to sing a song that

[40]*Against the Stream, op. cit.,* p. 116.
[41]*The Christian Century,* January 2, 1953, p. 7.

the roaring lions in the East and in the West cannot hear. How could they hear it!"[42]

While there are serious limitations in each of the above theologians' thought about communism, certain elements may be synthesized into a more realistic theological and ethical answer to the problem. Charles West has written a brilliant book in which he attempts such a synthesis.[43] Barth, he notes, provides the most devastating attack on all human ideologies and grounds Christian faith and practice in a radical christological theology. Barth's answers to communist ideology and all other ideologies is revelation. His point of departure is the concrete God who reveals himself in Christ. In answer to the communist view of history, which has to do with the response to forces in history, known and controlled by man, Barth makes time and history descriptive categories of what God is doing among men in Jesus Christ.[44] At the same time he lays emphasis upon hope, pointing Christians beyond religious thought to response to and hope in a concrete Lord of history.

But Barth never adequately integrates his theology with politics. His "neutralism" with reference to communist totalitarianism urging the church to "stand quietly aloof" and tread the narrow path midway between Moscow and Rome is puzzling in the light of the fact that he was violently opposed to Nazi totalitarianism and urged the church to take a stand against it.

Professor West finds Barth poorly informed about communism and guilty of "ineptitude . . . in the field of social and political decision."[45] Hence, West thinks that Barth requires the political insights of the American theologian, Reinhold Niebuhr, who in turn requires the theology of Barth. According to West: "Niebuhr's concentration on the facts of human political experience themselves, and his theology of continuing tension between love and law in political decision, compel him to take the realities of human social experience in all their complexity with a seri-

[42]*How to Serve God in a Marxist Land*, op. cit., p. 81.

[43]*Communism and the Theologians: Study of An Encounter*. Philadelphia: Westminster Press, 1958.

[44]*Ibid.*, pp. 351-352.

[45]*Ibid.*, p. 304.

ousness which Barth's theology allows, to be sure, but does not compel."[46] Barth's theology, therefore, fails to place the whole political process under the order of redemption, as seen in his inability to see the Soviets as a righteous or an unrighteous state. Nor does he directly relate his prophetic insights to communist oppression and its threat to the church and the free world.

On the other hand, Niebuhr lacks the profound theological basis for social ethics which Barth enjoys. He finds his ethical-social imperatives in history instead of the individual's relation to Christ. Once he saw in Marxism an instrument of Christian social ethics; now he attempts to find God's will in pragmatic, democratic tradition. Thus his ethic is largely derived from concrete historical situations, specifically in the balancing of power against power, always under the criticism of Christian love. And, as West notes, he has little to offer in the way of help for Christians in communist countries who have no power. Nor does he emphasize the Christian's personal witness to communists, but lays stress on the political factor.[47]

West goes on to say that Dietrich Bonhoeffer's theology can be used to synthesize an adequate theological approach to communism, though his encounter was with Nazism rather than communism.[48] Bonhoeffer, a student of both Barth and Niebuhr, lays emphasis upon the "mature world," a world come of age in organizational, rational, and technical competence. It is a world which has become nonreligious, in the sense that God is no longer necessary as a working hypothesis, whether in morals, politics, or science.[49] Neither Barth nor Brunner, according to West, understands the extent to which this mature, secular world is a reality. Niebuhr attempts to build contacts and emphasizes the need for revelation out of the dialectical encounter between moral reason and practical choices, and against the best reorientation of theological concepts, which remains in the realm of words in the case of Barth. Bonhoeffer

[46]Ibid., p. 313.
[47]Ibid., pp. 174-175.
[48]Ibid., p. 340.
[49]Prisoner for God. New York: Macmillan Co., 1953, p. 163.

stresses the insight that the maturity of this organized, technical world, within the limits of its own relative problem-solving concerns, is a fact of God's providence in our time, before which revolutionary impulses and Christian apologetics alike must show the respect which reality sooner or later demands of everyone.

Bonhoeffer's answer combines the adequacy of Niebuhr and Barth. As West declares:

> Christ reveals to us God's love, God's being and act, in the middle of this secular mature world, upholding it by his Providence in its relativity, its uncertainty, its temptation, reconciling it to himself out of its sin and rebellion. Reality is not to be found on the boundaries of this world, in those questions which it cannot answer and for which it therefore calls on the hypothesis God, nor in those failures and conflicts which it cannot resolve which drive it in despair to call on some transcendent help. It is not some explanation of the relations between a divine and a human realm. It is the reality of God who has come into this world in Jesus Christ, and the reality of this world as so loved by God.[50]

The response of the above theologians may give us some guidelines in our efforts to meet the communist challenge. The kind of theological posture which is demanded and which must be developed will involve: a renewed emphasis upon the sovereignty of God, the providence of God, a realistic view of history, man, sin, and society. Also it will be a theology which has relevance for the crucial political, economic, and social issues of our time. In short, it will be a theological ethic which is Biblically grounded, theologically meaningful, and socially relevant.

[50]*Op. cit.*, p. 343.

CHAPTER VII

Guidelines for Christian Action

Christianity in its historical pilgrimage has confronted numerous foes, From the very beginning, the primitive church was threatened by isms which sought to emasculate its distinctive mission and message or to totally destroy it outright. Among these ideologies and movements were Gnosticism, Marcionism, Manichaeism, and Islamism. Today other formidable foes threaten the church in terms of rationalism, materialism, secularism, scientism, and communism.

I. The Challenge of Communism

Contemporary communism is one of the most powerful forces ever to challenge the Christian faith. It is adamantly opposed to all religions, especially Christianity. Through its ideology, strategy, tactics, and propaganda, communism challenges Christianity at several levels. This chapter is concerned with the challenge of communism to Christianity and Christianity's response.

1. The Challenge of Communism as a Rival Faith

It is not only at the level of action, but basically at the level of faith that communism presents its greatest challenge to Christianity. Communism is fundamentally a secular religion. It has been called "a Christian heresy" and "the one living religion in the world today." As such, communism aims to stamp out the Christian faith because, in the words of Nicolas Berdyaev: "It wants to be a religion itself, to take the place of Christianity."[1]

As a secular faith, communism claims to have all the answers to the spiritual questions of the soul and provide the real meaning of life. To achieve its aims as a secular faith, communism provides counterparts of the essential doctrines of Christi-

[1]*The Origin of Russian Communism.* Ann Arbor: University of Michigan Press, 1960, p. 158.

anity. The personal God of creation becomes impersonal matter in motion, dialectically directed; Marx, Lenin, and Stalin become the prophets of the new religion; exploitation becomes original sin; revolution becomes the medium of redemption; the Party, with its discipline, becomes the church; the proletariat becomes the "Chosen People"; the overthrow of the capitalist and the enthronement of the worker replaces the judgment of God; and the classless society on earth takes the place of the Kingdom of God.

The communists also have their own set of the Ten Commandments. The new *Manual for Godless Youth,* re-edited from the 1947 original, is now being distributed in the Soviet Union. The commandments are stated as follows:

1. Remember that the clergy, regardless of faith, is the foremost enemy of our communist state.
2. Thou shalt labor diligently to draw thy friends and acquaintances toward communism, never forgetting that the Communist Party is the supreme authority of the atheist of the whole world.
3. Teach thy friends to shun all priests.
4. Guard thyself against spies, condemn saboteurs.
5. Busy thyself in the propagation of anti-religious magazines and newspapers.
6. Let every faithful communist be also a militant and forthright atheist.
7. Thou shalt resist religious ideas, always and everywhere, protecting thy friends from them.
8. The faithful atheist is likewise a goodly policeman, ever watchful of the security of the communist state.
9. Give generously of what thou hast to carry on missionary work among the unenlightened, especially outside the Soviet Union where atheism suffers underground.
10. Remember that if thou be not a devoted atheist, thou canst not be a faithful communist or even a firm Soviet citizen on whom our state can rely. Atheism and communism are of one bond, and these ideals are the foundations of Soviet power.

Mr. Ulbricht, communist boss of East Germany, has produced his own set of commandments. His ten commandments are:

1. Thou shalt devote thyself to the international solidarity of the working class, all working people, and to the unbreakable alliance of the socialist nations.

2. Thou shalt love thy fatherland and be prepared to devote all thy power and capabilities to the defense of the worker's and farmer's might.

3. Thou shalt help eliminate the exploitation of men by men.

4. Thou shalt perform good deeds for socialism, knowing that socialism leads to a better life for all working people.

5. Thou shalt perform in the spirit of mutual help in comradely collaboration for the construction of socialism, taking to heart the respecting collective criticism.

6. Thou shalt guard and increase the property of the people.

7. Thou shalt strive for the improvement of thy work, be economical, and strengthen socialist working discipline.

8. Thou shalt educate thy children in the spirit of peace and socialism, steeling their character and bodily development.

9. Thou shalt dwell cleanly and properly, respecting thy family.

10. Thou shalt declare thy solidarity with the people fighting for national liberation and national independence.

Mr. Ulbricht declared that these are the commandments for the new socialist ethic and a firm part of the communist world outlook.

In addition to secular doctrines and commandments, a liturgical movement is developing in communism. Communist ceremonies are taking the place of Christian rites in an attempt to eliminate the supernatural from all forms of popular Christian practices such as baptism, confirmation, marriage and funeral rites. For example, a name-giving ceremony is substituted for the baptism of infants. Parents swear that the newborn will be brought up as good socialists and the child is given a communist godfather. Also there is an effort to give marriage ceremonies a greater dignity. Marriage parlors have been established and orchestras are employed to play national classics for communist marriage ceremonies. All of these liturgies are designed to raise up a godless people in a godless society.

Thus communism attempts to be a complete coherent faith. In a sense communism is a secularization of the Judeo-Christian faith. And its dynamic is not in its materialism or even economics, but in its appeal as a total way of life. For it claims to have not only the religious answers to man's questions but also the only scientific answer to the problem of man and society.

2. The Communist Challenge of Education

A system of indoctrination has been developed in the USSR on such a vast scale as to stagger the imagination. Every farm and factory has its school for this purpose. Popular magazines, periodicals, pamphlets, newspapers, novels, books of all kinds are printed by the millions and made available at low cost. All mass media—radio, T.V., movies, etc.—trumpet the communist doctrines day and night.

Prior to the communist revolution in 1917, over half of the people in Russia could neither read nor write. Today illiteracy is practically nil. The public schools and universities are exacting and rigorous in demands on the student, and the whole educational system is oriented in the direction of communist goals.

One of the smartest things the communists have ever done was to bring thousands of students from all over the world to study in their schools. For years thousands of young people from all over the earth have taken advantage of a free education in the USSR and the other countries behind the Iron Curtain. Recently 3,000 scholarships were granted by Khrushchev to students in South America. The Soviets pay all expenses, give a check to each student at the end of the month, and all that is required of them is to return to their native country after six years of study. It is no accident that the leaders of revolutions in numerous countries today received their education on scholarships offered by communist schools.

3. The Communist Challenge of Evangelism

The communists have a strong evangelistic passion. Their evangelistic zeal stems from the fact that they believe that they hold the hope of the world in their hands. Joseph Stalin declared that "Outside socialism there is no salvation." Personal evangelism is one of the most effective methods of the communists. Traveling in Russia, the writer was constantly the object of evangelism by communist guides and officials. Hour after

hour and day after day, the communists talked incessantly
about their doctrines and way of life. One cannot help but
admire their persistence in preaching their doctrine. And one
is made to wonder how long the average Christian could discuss
his faith.

4. The Communist Challenge of Missions

Communism has a "Great Commission" which is taken quite
seriously. Compare the last paragraph of the Gospel of Matthew
with the last paragraph of the *Communist Manifesto*, the "creed"
of the communists. It states in part: "The communists disdain
to conceal their views and aims . . . the proletarians have
nothing to lose but their chains. They have a world to win."

Thus the communists have a *weltanschauung*, a world view.
They are out to communize every nation on the globe. Their
mission program is on a massive and gigantic scale. Thousands
of trained persons stand ready to enter any country which
calls for Soviet help. Many thousands of others penetrate into
countries without invitation with the view to communizing
them. It is estimated that one out of every three-hundred-and-
fifty Russians is trained for service in other countries of the
world.

5. The Challenge of Social Action

Communism aims to change the world. Karl Marx declared:
"Philosophers have only *interpreted* the world in various ways;
the point, however, is to *change* it." Hence communism is no
mere theory, but demands a radical reconstruction of all society
in terms of the socialistic pattern. Mere amelioration of the ills
of a capitalistic society is repugnant to the communist. Improvements within a democratic society are not enough. The total
system must be transformed in terms of the communist pattern.
To accomplish this, every technique—the big lie, intrigue, revolution, murder, enslavement, torture, propaganda, and brute force
—is put into action. Communists claim that the whole world will
be communistic in the next two decades. At the Twenty-Second
Congress of the Communist Party of the Soviet Union, Khrush-

chev gave a blueprint for communizing the world in the next twenty years.

6. The Communist Challenge of Consecration

Complete dedication to the cause of communism is demanded of every Party member. For the devoted communist, no sacrifice is too great and no service too small. A former missionary to China relates how he saw Chinese students, sons and daughters of wealthy parents, put on tattered garments and go out among the millions of miserable poverty-ridden people, teaching and preaching the gospel of communism. When one of these students was led before the Nationalist government firing squad, her last words were: "I die for a cause. You have nothing for which to live." It is tragic to see communists who are so whole-hearted for a half-truth and Christians who are so half-hearted for the whole truth!

II. The Christian Response

How shall the Christian forces meet the communist challenge? Certainly Christians must do more than merely criticize communism. Hurling verbal condemnations and exhortations will not solve the problem. Communism cannot be wished away nor will it collapse by calling it bad names. In approaching the issue of communism, Christians must be more than *anti*-communist. This is the negative approach. There are positive ways of meeting the communist conspiracy, and there are practical guidelines in this direction.

1. Theological Renewal

The core of the conflict between Christianity and communism lies in the area of ideology. Communist philosophy must be answered at the theological level or at the level of basic Christian truth. As Gerald Kennedy has so well said: "If the struggle is merely political, then we may expect the State Department to save us. If it is economic we may trust the National Association of Manufacturers to lead us. If it is military, then the Pentagon will give the orders. But if it is essentially a spiritual-moral conflict, then the Christian Church must be held responsible for the outcome."[2]

To strike at the root from which communism grows, the church must provide a theological answer to Marxist ideology. All other attacks will be secondary and fail to hit the heartbeat of the lifeblood of communism. Christian theology should be aimed so as to pierce the ideological armor of the communist himself and to provide a convincing answer to his materialistic and utopian views of history, man, economics, and society. At this point the encounters of those theologians who have had a living theological response to communism may give guidance in the development of a Christian theological stance, *vis-à-vis* that problem.

2. The Church and Genuine Repentance

The Christian church must approach the problem of communism in the spirit of repentance. Communism may be a symbol of judgment for a lack of prophetic spirit and concern for social justice on the part of the church. God has used pagan forces before to mediate his judgment. Isaiah, the prophet, said that Assyria's oppression of Israel was God's judgment against the sinful people (Isaiah 10:5). Communism could be a rebuke to the churches for entanglement with the world; for involvement in forms of economic and racial injustice which have created conditions for the growth of communism. Far too often Christianity has been used to justify the humiliation of people and to defend economic, political, and social oppression. The church must repent and become the vanguard of social justice. Christian concern for social welfare must be greater than that of the communists. Christian practice of freedom, equality, and justice is the way to defeat communists who promise these in theory but deny them in practice.

3. Recapture Revolutionary Christianity

The early church was revolutionary. It was accused of turning the world "upside down" (Acts 17:6-7). Elton Trueblood has

[2]"Defender and Invader," *Christianity Today*, December 21, 1962, p. 9.

said: "Once a church was a brave and revolutionary fellowship, changing the course of history . . . today it is a place where people go and sit on comfortable benches, waiting patiently until the time to go home for their Sunday dinners."[3]

Today the church has lost much of its revolutionary thrust. Frequently it tends to be more molded by culture than a molder of culture. It has too often stood for the status quo or society-in-itself. Around the world the churches and the clergy have tended to side with the "haves" against the "have nots." This was one of the major reasons why the churches were repudiated in Russia and why a country where 90 per cent of the population belongs to churches falls like ripe fruit into the communist camp. In these nations the churches failed to challenge economic distress, poverty, disease, and ignorance of the suffering masses. Hence the people were easy prey to communist ideology which professed to bring them a better way of life. Unfortunately the impression has been left with the masses of the people that churches have little more to offer them than mere "pie in the sky" when they die. Jesus came that men might have life and have it "more abundantly," and this includes physical necessities which make for a richer and fuller life. The church is more than an ambulance corps to pick up the crushed and wounded. It must seek to prevent the evil forces in society from crushing and wounding humanity.

4. Inner Personal Discipline

The time has come for the Christian to exemplify in his own life the spirit and ethic of Jesus. This will involve inner personal discipline. The renewal of the Christian community will come about only as its members engage in prayer, study, and the discipline of the Christian life in the world. Christian personal living is the most potent witness to communists. One's life always speaks much louder than his words. Inner discipline of life is the only way that we can hope to overcome our obsession for material success, passion for pleasure, spiritual insensitivity, and moral flabbiness.

[3]*Alternative to Futility.* New York: Harper and Brothers, 1948, p. 31.

5. Serious Study of Communism

It is imperative that the Christian study the problem of communism. A thorough knowledge of the nature, aims, and tactics of communism is essential to meeting its challenge. Action against communism must be based on information rather than emotion. Numerous anti-communist movements are springing up across the country, but too often they generate more emotional fervor than the presentation of real facts about the communist conspiracy. A thorough knowledge about the strength and weakness of communism is the effective way of dealing with this issue. Solid books are available on the subject, such as the following: R. N. Carew Hunt, *The Theory and Practice of Communism*, New York: Macmillan Company, 1961; John C. Bennett, *Christianity and Communism Today*, New York: Association Press, 1960; J. Edgar Hoover, *Masters of Deceit*, New York: Henry Holt, Company, 1958; Ralph Lord Roy, *Communism and the Churches*, New York: Harcourt, Brace, and Company, 1960; and Lester DeKoster, *Communism and Christian Faith*, Grand Rapids: Wm. B. Eerdmans Publishing Co., 1962. In addition to these works see the bibliography of this book.

There is little to fear if a free people thoroughly understand contemporary communism, for they will never fall for its line. A study program should be drafted and set in motion by every religious denomination to examine and expose the demonic nature of Marxist communism.

6. Christian Evangelism

To meet the communist challenge we must recover the evangelistic zeal of primitive Christianity. Against almost insuperable difficulties early Christians went forth to win the world to Christ. These Christians had a passion for souls which impelled them to "become all things to all men" that they might win others to Christ. Paul declared: "Brethren, my heart's desire and prayer to God for Israel is, that they might be saved" (Romans 10:1). Early Christians "went everywhere preaching the word" (Acts 8:4).

Baptists in Russia, in spite of persecution, demonstrate the kind of courage and personal evangelism that is often lacking among Christians in America. An article in a recent issue of the *Komsomolskaja Pravda,* official paper of the Communist Youth Organization, stamps the Baptists as particularly dangerous, for among them the laymen are evangelists. The paper complains, "Every Baptist tries to win at least one adherent to his faith."[4]

Many leading theologians who have dealt with the communist problem have often completely neglected personal evangelism in relation to individual communists. Communists know the value of personal evangelism and practice it with zeal. Christians would do well to make more of personal witness to the individual. This means that the Christian will take responsibility for his witness and will travail with individuals until Christ "be formed" in them.

7. Missionary Outreach

Communists take seriously their call to world missions as seen in the fact that they are out to communize every country. Almost a half-million persons trained in communist "missions" are now in Africa and Asia. Almost one-third of the earth's population is now in the communist camp.

Jesus gave the disciples a Great Commission: "Go therefore and make disciples of all nations" (Matthew 28:19). Christians have not taken this mandate seriously enough. After almost 2,000 years, Christianity has fewer followers than communism.

This makes one wonder if Christians really believe in missions. The per member figure for giving to foreign missions among thirty-nine Protestant bodies in this country is only $2.04.[5]

To meet the demand of the Great Commission and the challenge of communist world missions, our missionary strategy must be modified and more adequately supported. Missions must become more than an extra-curricular activity in our churches. Indeed, missions must become the central thrust of our faith and action.

[4]*The Baptist World,* Vol. 5, No. 2, February, 1958, p. 4.
[5]*Yearbook of American Churches.* Edited by Benson Y. Landis. New York: National Council of Churches of Christ in the U.S.A., p. 272, 1963.

Protestant missionaries sent out from all countries of the world number less than 43,000. Less than 28,000 represent North American foreign missions. Southern Baptists, ten-million strong, have fewer than 1,600 foreign missionaries. Only 2,820 have been appointed since 1845. Communist agents now serving communism in all parts of the world far outnumber all Protestant missionaries combined.

Communists are making it increasingly difficult for the Christian world mission program. In Asia, thousands of missionaries have been accused of being foreign agents of American imperialism and have been driven out of many countries. Hundreds of churches have been closed, and those that remain open are forbidden to accept any support from foreign mission boards. No missionaries are allowed to be sent into countries dominated by the communists and the churches are cut off from the outside world.

Christian missionaries from America once had a privileged position among the blacks and the orientals. Now the communists have engendered hatred among the people toward our country and missionaries find themselves being charged as agents of colonial powers and exploiting imperialistic America. Thus the time has come when the missionary can no longer hold a patronizing air, defend the doctrine of white supremacy, and expect to win people in Africa and Asia to Christianity and to a democratic way of life.

Here at home we hamper the missionary effort in Africa by our unjust treatment of Negroes in terms of discrimination and segregation. In a letter to a denominational paper, a missionary from Nigeria commenting on the racial explosion at "Old Miss" University at Oxford, Mississippi, observed: "You are closing the door of Africa in our faces. The communists do not need to work against the preaching of the gospel here by Americans; you are doing it quite adequately. Wake up!"[6]

In terms of a new strategy, the churches must send out an increasing number of missionaries from America who possess technical skills to help the people help themselves toward a better economic, political, and social life. Recently a judge and

[6]*The Baptist Record,* November 15, 1962, p. 4.

a state senator from North Carolina made public his decision to become a foreign missionary of the Methodist Church, and is now serving in Southern Rhodesia. Likewise the president of the Baptist Brotherhood of Louisiana, a civil engineer, was appointed to Korea as a missionary by the Southern Baptist Foreign Mission Board. We must no longer look upon the missionary as only preachers, but as doctors, nurses, contractors, sanitation experts, farm specialists, and others similarly qualified to serve on mission fields.

8. Building Bridges of Fellowship

Christians in this country must build bridges of love and understanding between themselves and people in all nations. One can personally correspond with people in many nations, and even in Russia. There are many Christians behind the Iron Curtain who long for fellowship with other Christians abroad. But one of the most effective ways that Christian churches can build bridges of understanding with people of other nations is by making it possible for young people of these countries to study in American schools and to visit in American homes. It is unfortunate that some Negro students have been rejected by Christian colleges in this country though they were academically qualified and even won to Christ by graduates of such institutions. Students go back to their native countries to become leaders in every area of life. Generally those trained in Christian colleges provide a stable and intelligent leadership for their respective countries. In contrast, for example, to the Belgian Congo situation, Nigeria is relatively stable and secure from communist inroads. This is due largely to the fact that the leadership of this newly independent country has been trained in Christian schools.

9. Responsible Citizenship

The Christian must act responsibly as a citizen in a free democratic society. He has the moral obligation to become informed about the nature and function of government, to work for the election of able political leaders, to strive for the enactment of just laws, and to participate in action for a righteous community.

Every Christian, regardless of his political leanings, should exercise his great heritage to vote at the polls. It is a national disgrace the way citizens of this country fail to cast their ballots on election day. Only 62 per cent of Americans of voting age cast their ballots in the 1956 presidential election, and only 43.6 per cent in the congressional election of 1958. These figures compare with the following percentages of voting in other Western countries: 90 per cent in Italy, 85 per cent in West Germany, 80 per cent in France and Britain. In the Soviet Union, where there is only one party which selects its own candidates, and where the people have the option to vote "yes" or "no," about 99.98 per cent vote and 99.99 per cent vote "yes."

Citizens who fail to exercise their rights to participate in the political life of our nation have little right to criticize political leaders or policies. For they themselves are responsible in a large measure for any sort of politcial situation that may exist.

As citizens, Christians can work through political channels to establish legislation which will provide "liberty and justice for all." Communism will have little chance for success in a country that moves steadily toward equal rights, decent living standards, and fair play for all citizens irrespective of color, culture, and creed.

10. Sursum Corda

In the light of the prevalent sense of defeat due to communist conquest, Christians should remember the invincible nature of the church. Jesus declared that "the gates [powers] of hell shall not prevail against it" (Matthew 16:18). All the isms and powers of the world cannot destroy Christ's church. Ultimately it will triumph through Christ over the "beast and the false prophets." The invincible nature of the church is symbolized in a church house which stands in the city of Warsaw, Poland. Destroyed by Hitler, it was rebuilt by devoted church members in spite of the current communist regime. On the facade of the building is inscribed the following statement: *"Sursum Corda."*

"Lift up your hearts!" Let the church lift up its heart in these times which try men's souls. Let the church hear the voice of the eternal as heard by the early Christians when the church was under terrible persecution: "Alleluia: for the Lord God omnipotent reigneth" (Revelation 19:6). Gripped by this conviction, the Christian forces will be more than conquerors through Christ.

The above suggestions are only a few ways in which Christian forces can positively meet the communist challenge. The time is short. Christians must put into practice what they profess to preach, namely, the gospel. Translated into action this gospel calls for the redemption of the individual and the reconstruction of society more in keeping with the principles of the Kingdom of God.

Bibliography

Primary Sources

Burns, Emil, *A Handbook of Marxism*. New York: Random House, 1935.

Daniels, Robert, *A Documentary History of Communism from Lenin to Mao*. New York: Random House, 1960.

Engels, Friedrich, *Anti-Duhring*. New York: International Publishers, 1937.

Feuer, Lewis S., ed., *Marx and Engels Basic Writings on Politics and Philosophy*. New York: Anchor Books, Doubleday, 1959.

Lenin, V. I., *Religion*. New York: International Publishers, 1933.

Little Lenin Library, 28 volumes. New York: International Publishers.

Marx, Karl, *Capital; The Communist Manifesto;* and *Other Writings*. New York: The Modern Library, 1932.

Mendel, A. P., *Essential Works of Marxism*. New York: Bantam Books, 1961.

Stalin, Joseph, *Dialectical and Historical Materialsm*, New York: International Publishers, 1940.

————, *Leninism: Selected Writings*. New York, 1942.

Interpretative, Analytical, Critical

Almond, Gabriel H., *The Appeals of Communism*. Princeton: Princeton University Press, 1954.

Bober, M. M., *Karl Marx's Interpretation of History*. Cambridge: Harvard University Press, 1927.

Burnham, J., *The Coming Defeat of Communism*. New York: Day, 1950.

Chambers, Whitaker, *I Was a Witness*. New York: Random House, 1952.

Crossman, R. H. S., ed., *The God That Failed*. New York: Macmillan, 1945.

Doerig, J. A., *Marx vs. Russia*. New York: Ungar, 1962.

Djilas, Milovan, *The New Class*. New York: Praeger, 1955.

Hunt, R. N. Carew, *Marxism Past and Present*. New York: Macmillan, 1955.

————, *The Theory and Practice of Communism*. New York: Macmillan, 1961.

————, *A Guide to Communist Jargon*. New York: Macmillan, 1957.

Overstreet, Harry A., *What We Must Know About Communism*. New York: Norton, 1958.

————, Harry and Bonaro, *The War Called Peace*. New York: Norton, 1961.

Strausz-Hupé, Robert, *et. al.*, *Protracted Conflict*. New York: Harper, 1959.

Biographies

Beer, Max, *The Life and Teaching of Karl Marx*. Boston: Small, Maynard, 1924.

Berlin, Isaiah, *Karl Marx*. Toronto: Nelson, 1939.

Carr, E. H., *Karl Marx*. London: Aldine House, 1938.

Deutscher, I., *Stalin: A Political Biography*. New York: Oxford University Press, 1949.

Mayer, Gustav, *Friedrich Engels*, New York: Knopf, 1936.

Ruhle, Otto, *Karl Marx: His Life and Work*. New York: Viking, 1929.

Shub, David, *Lenin: A Biography*. New York: Doubleday, 1948.

Trotsky, Leon, *Stalin: An Appraisal of the Man and His Influence*. New York: Grossett and Dunlap, 1941.

Wolf, B. D., *Three Who Made a Revolution*. New York: Dial 1948.

Communism in Russia

Berdyaev, Nicolas, *The Origin of Russian Communism*. Ann Arbor: University of Michigan Press, 1960.

Conybeare, Frederick C., *Russian Dissenters*, New York: Russell and Russell, 1962 (Harvard Theological Studies).

Dallin, D. Y., *The Real Soviet Russia*. New Haven: Yale University Press, 1944.

Reed, John, *Ten Days That Shook the World.* New York: Vantage Books, Random House, 1961.

Salvidori, Massimo, *The Rise of Modern Communism.* New York: Holt, 1952.

Spinka, Matthew, *The Church in Soviet Russia.* New York: Oxford University Press, 1956.

The Spread of Communism

Alexander, Robert, *Communism in Latin America.* New Brunswick, New Jersey: Rutgers University Press, 1957.

Brandt, Conrad, *et. al., A Documentary History of Chinese Communism.* Cambridge: Harvard University Press, 1952.

Draper, Theodore, *Castro's Revolution: Myths and Realities.* New York: Praeger, 1962.

Hughes, John, *The New Face of Africa.* New York: Longman's, Green, 1961.

Schwarts, B., *Chinese Communism and the Rise of Mao.* Cambridge: Harvard University Press, 1951.

Seton-Watson, Hugh, *The East European Revolution,* New York: Praeger, 1953.

Tang, Peter, *Communist China Today.* New York: Praeger, 1960.

Communism in American Life

Draper, Theodore, *The Roots of American Communism.* New York: Harcourt, Brace, 1957.

————, *American Communism and Soviet Power.* New York: Harcourt, Brace, 1960.

Foster, William Z., *History of the Communist Party in the United States.* New York: International Publishers, 1960.

Hoover, J. Edgar, *Masters of Deceit: The Story of Communism in America and How to Fight It.* New York: Holt, 1958.

Howe, Irwin, and Coser, Lewis, *The American Communist Party —A Critical History 1919-1957.* Boston: Beacon, 1958.

Iverson, Robert W., *The Communists and the Schools.* New York: Harcourt, Brace, 1959.

Kampleman, Max, *The Communist Party vs. The CIO.,* Praeger 1957.

Palmer, Edward D., ed., *The Communist Problem in America: A Book of Readings.* New York: Thomas Y. Crowell, 1951.

Randall, Clarence B., *The Communist Challenge to American Business*. Boston: Little, Brown, 1959

Record, Wilson, *The Negro and the Communist Party*. Chapel Hill: University of North Carolina Press, 1951.

Rossi, A., *A Communist Party in Action*. New Haven: Yale University Press, 1949.

Rossiter, Clinton, *Marxism: The View from America*. New York: Harcourt, Brace, 1960.

Shannon, David, *The Decline of American Communism*. New York: Harcourt, Brace, 1959.

Spolarsky, Jacob, *The Communist Trail in America*. New York: Macmillan, 1951.

Saposs, David Joseph, *Communism in American Politics*. Public Affairs, 1960.

Ethics of Communism

Barnette, H. H., "Communist and Christian Ethics," *Review and Expositor*, Vol. LIII, No. 31, July, 1956.

Lowrie, Donald A., "Dialectic Morality," *Religion in Life*, Vol. XXV, No. 2, Spring, 1956.

Nivison, David S., *Communist Ethics and Chinese Tradition*. Cambridge: M.I.T., 1954.

Selsom, Howard, *Socialism and Ethics*. New York: International Press, 1943.

Shishkin, A., *The Basis of Communist Morality*. Moscow: State Publishing House of Political Literature, 1955.

Trotsky, Leon, *Their Morals and Ours*. New York: Pioneer Publishers, 1942.

Christianity and Communism

Bach, Marcus, *God and the Soviets*. New York: Thomas Y. Crowell, 1958.

Bales, James D., *Communism: Its Faith and Fallacies*. Grand Rapids, Mich.: Baker Book House, 1962.

Barron, J. B., and Waddams, H. M., *Communism and the Churches*. New York: Morehouse-Gorham, 1950.

Barth, Karl, *How to Serve God in a Marxist Land*. New York: Association Press, 1959.

Bennett, John C., *Christianity and Communism Today*. New York: Association Press, 1960.

Berdyaev, Nicholas, *Christianity and Class War*. New York: Sheed and Ward, 1933.

Blanchard, Paul, *Communism, Democracy and Catholic Power*. Boston: Beacon, 1951.

Bolshakoff, Serge, *The Christian Church and the Soviet State*. New York: Macmillan, 1942.

Braden, Charles S., *War, Communism and World Religions*. New York: Harper, 1953.

Brown, William N., *Communism and Christianity*. Galion, Ohio: Bradford-Brown, 1920.

Brunner, Emil, *Communism, Capitalism, Christianity*. London: Lutterworth Press, 1949.

Buber, Martin, *Paths to Utopia*. London: Routledge and Kegan Paul, 1949.

Butler, J. F., *Communism and Christianity*. Madras, India: The Christian Literature Society for India, 1949.

Casserley, J. V. H., *The Bent World*. New York: Oxford University Press, 1955.

Cianfarra, C. M., *The Vatican and the Kremlin*. New York: Dutton, 1950.

Committee on World Literacy, *A Christian's Handbook on Communism*. New York: Committee on World Literacy and Christian Literature. 1962.

Cronin, John F., *Communism: Threat to Freedom*. Washington: National Catholic Welfare Conference, 1962.

Curtis, John S., *Church and State in Russia: The Last Years of the Empire, 1900-1917*. New York: Columbia University Press, 1940.

————, *The Russian Church and the Soviet State, 1917-1950*. New York: Macmillan, 1953.

DeKoster, Lester, *Communism and Christian Faith*. Grand Rapids, Michigan: Eerdmans, 1962.

Drewett, John, *Communism*, Edinburgh: Edinburgh House Press, Eton Gate, 1953.

Dufay, Francis, *Red Star Versus the Cross*. London: Paternoster Press, 1954.

Fedotov, G. P., *The Russian Church and the Revolution.* New York: Macmillian, 1948.

Feuerbach, Ludwig, *The Essence of Christianity.* Trans. by George Eliot. New York: Harper, 1957.

Galter, Albert, *The Red Book of the Persecuted Church* (2nd edition). Westminister, Maryland: Newman, 1957.

Geren, Paul, *Christians Confront Communism.* Nashville: Convention Press, 1962.

Gollwitzer, Helmut, *Unwilling Journey. A Diary from Russia.* S.C.M., 1957.

Harris, Henry W., ed., *Christianity and Communism.* New York: Oxford University Press, 1937, Boston: Marshall Jones Co., 1937, Contributors: Inge, Barry, Niebuhr, *et al.*

Hecker, J F., *Religion and Communism.* New York: Wylie, 1934.

Heimann, Eduard, "A Christian Looks at Communism," Chapter III, *The Christian Demand for Social Justice* (Edited by Bishop William Scarlett) New York: The New American Library of World Literature, Inc, 1949.

Hordern, William, *Christianity, Communism and History.* New York: Abingdon, 1954.

James, H. Ingli, *Communism and Christian Faith.* London: The Carey Kingsgate Press, Ltd., 1950.

Jeffreys, M. B. C., *The Kingdom of This World: The Challenge of Communism.* London and Oxford: A. R. Mowbray, Ltd., 1950.

Jones, E. Stanley, *Christ's Alternative to Communism.* New York: Abingdon, 1935.

Jones, Francis Price, *The Church in Communist China: A Protestant Appraisal.* New York: Friendship, 1962.

Kautsky, Karl, *Foundations of Christianity,* Trans. by Henry F. Mins. New York: S. A. Russell, 1953.

Lewis, John, ed., *Christianity and Social Revolution.* London: V. Gollarcz, 1935.

Lowry, Charles W., *Communism and Christ.* New York: Morehouse-Gorham, 1952.

MacKinnon, D. M., ed., *Christian Faith and Communist Faith.* New York: St. Martin's Press, 1953.

Maritain, Jacques, *True Humanism.* New York: Scribner's, 1938.

Miller, Alexander, *The Christian Significance of Karl Marx*. New York: Macmillan, 1949.

Myers, Edward D., "The Soviet Challenge to Christianity," *Theology Today*, Vol. 2:496-512.

Nersoyan, Tiran, *A Christian Approach to Communism*. London: Frederick Muller, Ltd., 1942.

Niebuhr, Reinhold, *The Children of Darkness and the Children of Light*. New York: Scribner's, 1950.

Nivison, David S., *Communist Ethics and Chinese Tradition*. Cambridge: Center of International Studies, Massachusetts Institute of Technology, 1954.

Pemberton, P. L., *Christians Face the Total Menace of Communism*. Philadelphia: Judson, 1962.

Pius XI, "Atheistic Communism" (*Divini Redemptoris*), in Husslein, Joseph, *Social Wellsprings*, Vol. II, p. 339-374. Milwaukee: Bruce, 1949.

Rehwinkel, Alfred M., *Communism and the Church*. St. Louis, Missouri: Concordia, 1948.

Rogers, Edward, *A Christian Commentary on Communism*. New York: Praeger, 1952.

Roy, Ralph Lord, *Communism and the Churches*. New York: Harcourt, Brace, 1960.

Ryan, John A., *Relation of Catholicism to Fascism, Communism and Democracy*. Washington: National Catholic Welfare Conference, 1938.

Saloff-Astakhoff, N. I., *Christianity in Russia*. New York: Larzeaux, 1941.

Shaffer, Walter T., *Russian Communism Vs. God's Communism: A Study of Opposites*. New York: William-Frederick, 1952.

Sheed, F. J., *Christianity and Communism*. New York: Sheed and Ward, 1938.

————, *Communism and the Conscience of the West*. Indianapolis: Bobbs-Merrill, 1947.

Shuster, George M., *Religion Behind the Iron Curtain*. New York: Macmillan, 1954.

Spinka, Matthew, *Christianity Confronts Communism*. New York: Harper, 1936.

————, *Church in Soviet Russia*. New York: Oxford University Press, 1956.

————, Church in Communist Society: *A Study in J. L. Hromadka's Theological Politics*. Hartford: Hartford Seminary Press, 1954.

————, *The Church and the Russian Revolution*. New York: Macmillan, 1927.

Stackwood, Mervyn, *Christianity and Marxism*. London: S.P.C.K., 1950.

Tobias, Robert, *Communist-Christian Encounter in East Europe*. Indianapolis: School of Religion Press, 1956.

Wood, H. G., *Christianity and Communism*. New York: Round Table, 1933.

Zernov, Nicolas, *The Russians and Their Church*. London: S.P.C.K., 1950.

INDEX